Celebrate
Marlborough
Sauvignon Blanc

IRVINE HOLT

Copyright © Belinda Jackson Wine Text
Copyright © Jan Bilton Recipes
Copyright © Jan Bilton Food Styling and Food Photography
Copyright © Kevin Judd Photography www.kevinjudd.co.nz – cover, pgs: 4/5, 11, 13, 68
Copyright © Winery images from specific wineries
Copyright © Irvine Holt Enterprises Ltd

Editor: Michael G. Ryan
Design: Debbie Morgan, Art Tank Ltd,
22 Kowhai Drive, Te Kouma, Coromandel, New Zealand.

First published in 2011
Publisher: Irvine Holt Enterprises Ltd,
PO Box 5183, Springlands, Blenheim 7241,
Marlborough, New Zealand
ph +64 3 579 6100

ISBN 978-0-9597594-6-4

Cover image: The Yarrum vineyard between the Brancott and Ben Morven Valleys.

Thanks to:
Wendy Inder: Kitchen assistance
Participating wineries
Regal Salmon: www.regalsalmon.co.nz for supplying salmon
Premium Game: www.game-meats.co.nz for supplying wild rabbit
Wine Marlborough: Marlborough Wine Trail map

Printed in China through Bookbuilders

Celebrate
Marlborough
Sauvignon Blanc

WINE Belinda Jackson
FOOD Jan Bilton

EDITOR MICHAEL G. RYAN
IRVINE HOLT

Contents

Cloudy Bay vineyard

The Sauvignon Blanc Story

Sauvignon blanc's origins can be traced back to 17th-century France. It has two 'homes' there – the Loire Valley towards the north-east of the country and Bordeaux in the south-west. In the Loire, the grape is found predominantly at the eastern end of this beautiful valley surrounding the hilltop village of Sancerre to the north of the Loire River and throughout Pouilly-sur-Loire just across the water to the south.

In Sancerre, sauvignon blanc is grown in soils mainly of limestone, Kimmeridgean marl, gravel and the famous flinty mineral deposits, also known as silex. The resulting wines are sinuous and fine with lifted, mineral aromatics and a nervy acidity. Their purity, freshness and more subtle fruit flavours makes them a highly popular food wine, a famed match for oysters in particular

Pouilly-fumé, the wine from Pouilly-sur-Loire, is so named after the mineral, flinty, aged soils, which give a particularly dominant smoky, or 'gun flint' character to the wines, hence the word 'fume' which is French for 'smoke' or 'smoky'.

Sauvignon blanc is responsible for the dry white wines of the Bordeaux region including Entre-Deux-Mers and Graves and is a vital component of the richly sweet and decadent wines of Sauternes, where it is blended with semillon in proportions from five to 50 per cent. These long-lived sweet wines can age gracefully for many years – the natural acidity of the semillon and sauvignon blanc acting as a kind of preservative while the rich fruit flavours and weighty textures evolve.

In North America, the grape found fame in the hands of Robert Mondavi in the late 1960s. He was offered a parcel of sauvignon blanc and finding it somewhat harsh with its prominent acidity and fresh, gooseberry-like flavours, he decided to age it in oak barrels to round it out and smooth the sharp edges. Christened fumé blanc (not to be confused with pouilly fumé from the Loire), the style became very popular.

Sauvignon blanc has limited importance in countries other than New Zealand. In Italy, it does well in the north-eastern region of Alto Adige while in Chile, the most successful area for this grape is Valparaiso. Australia has had success with sauvignon blanc in cool climate areas such as South Australia's Adelaide Hills and Padthaway and Margaret River in Western Australia, though in many parts of the country it is blended with semillon to give a heavier style of dry white wine. In South Africa, sauvignon blanc is a significant grape in the cooler regions of Stellenbosch and Durbanville. South Africa is currently the third largest producer of sauvignon blanc behind France and New Zealand.

Sauvignon Blanc in New Zealand

When it comes to wine production and sauvignon blanc in particular, New Zealand punches way above its weight. From some trial plantings in Marlborough dotted amongst the abundant müller-thurgau and riesling, sauvignon blanc was first planted seriously by Montana (now Brancott Estate) in the seventies, leading to their first release in 1979. Though more extensive plantings weren't undertaken until the mid-eighties, the sauvignon blanc grape had made its mark and there was no turning back.

Though Marlborough is the focus for sauvignon blanc in New Zealand, other regions are more than deserving of a mention. Hawke's Bay has produced sauvignon blanc for many years, the wines tending to be riper in style, more tropical and heavier than their South Island counterparts. Elsewhere in the North Island, Martinborough makes fresh, inviting styles and has a climate not dissimilar to that of Marlborough. Waipara, a region along the east coast of the South Island (south of Kaikoura and north of Christchurch) makes some excellent styles together with a range of other aromatics while Central Otago also makes top-notch sauvignon blancs, particularly from producers such as Peregrine, Coal Pit and Rippon.

Marlborough's Subregions

Marlborough has to date, tended to be thought of as just one fairly generic region because that is how it has primarily been promoted. There are in fact three distinct subregions and further smaller areas within each one. The idea that an area the size of Marlborough could be consistent in soils, climate and topography is perhaps as illogical as thinking that all sauvignon blancs taste the same.

The subregions from north to south are Wairau, encompassing Renwick, Rapaura, Conders Bend, Kaituna, Lower Wairau, Dillons Point, Grovetown and Rarangi. Then the Southern Valleys which include Brancott, Waihopai, Ben Morvern, Fairhall and Omaka. Thirdly, the Awatere Valley south of the township of Blenheim includes Redwood Pass, Blind River and Seaview.

Wines from the subregions have individual styles and can perhaps have their key characteristics described as follows: Wairau Valley – guava and passionfruit spectrum, but also a mineral, fine-bodied character. The Southern Valleys' wines show more bell-pepper, gooseberry and cut-grass flavours with a richness and weight on the palate. The Awatere Valley offers wines which display a racier, more herbaceous character often with a nettle and tomato leaf, almost stalky note, then a ripe, fruit-sweetness on the palate. There are also more complex and refined styles of sauvignon blancs with a greater level of winemaking treatment. This includes wild ferment, barrel ferment, lees stirring, oak ageing and/or blending with semillon to help achieve a less overt, more refined, but complex style which has the ability to age. The trick is to create a wine of deep complexity but ensure it still has relevance to its origin.

These described styles are somewhat general as much depends on individual vineyard sites and when the grapes are picked.

Today's wines still tend to be labelled 'Marlborough' but more and more producers are now labelling their wine with the name of the subregion to give that all important point of difference. Wines labelled 'Marlborough' can be a blend of grapes from any of the three subregions, though naming a wine as 'Awatere' for example, means that the grapes must come predominantly from that subregion. With such different styles from each area, wine shops and restaurants around the world will soon be acknowledging the importance of offering wines from each of these regions if they wish to accurately represent Marlborough to their clientele.

The Different Styles

The key difference inherent in wines of the same grape variety is where they are grown. Different soil types are perhaps the most influential, swiftly followed by climate – temperatures and hours of sunlight, humidity, rain and every other element. Site also plays a part – if the vineyard is on a north-facing slope, then this will tend to be warmer than a south-facing slope. Vine age and vineyard practices also have a strong influence.

Man of course has the ability to manipulate and manage many aspects in order to influence wine style, both in the vineyard and in the winery. A great job in the vineyard should lead to minimal intervention by the winemaker, merely caretaking the grapes from vine to bottle in the hope of accurately expressing the grapes' origin. Sauvignon blanc is a relatively straightforward wine to make, requiring cool temperatures and stainless steel tanks for fermentation. This is rather a generalisation as many wines will undergo different methods depending on the desired style, but for the most part, it is a simple process.

A key aspect of the aromas and flavours of sauvignon blanc and in particular Marlborough sauvignon blanc, is the balance of methoxypyrazines and thiols. This may sound technical and complicated but simply put, they are compounds that influence whether the wine will be overtly herbaceous with pungent green capsicum aromas or more of a tropical style with passionfruit characters. Winemakers, of course, have a preference for their style of wine and have loyal customers who love them for it, though it is always a delicate balancing act, particularly having the vagaries of Mother Nature to contend with each year.

In a nutshell, methoxypyrazines start to develop once the grape berries form and then decline just prior to veraison (this is when the grapes start to ripen and change colour). The thiols are also present in the grapes but are odourless until their characters are released during the fermentation process by enzymes in the yeast. When making sauvignon blanc, winemakers tend to want thiols to contribute passionfruit, gooseberry and/or blackcurrant aromas. But if the concentrations are too great, the aromas can be reminiscent of sweat or body odour – not quite so attractive!

Classic Marlborough sauvignon blanc is often a blend from two or all three of the subregions and could be described as zesty with a crisp acidity and pungent, passionfruit and other tropical fruit flavours, as well as red pepper (bell pepper/capsicum), gooseberry with fresh herbal characters.

The Vineyard
Winter

The vineyard year starts (or ends, depending on how you look at it) with pruning, often done soon after harvest. The method by which the vines are pruned will influence the yield and quality by determining how the vine grows.

Prior to pruning, the vine is a mass of branches, or canes as they are called. Two, three or four will have been laid along the fruiting wires for the current year's fruit and the job now is for a skilled vineyard manager to select the canes for the following year and remove all the others. He or she will tend each vine selecting the canes they want to keep and cutting the others off at the base, close to the head of the vine.

Next, the canes that have been cut need to be removed. Often a manual job, workers go through the vineyard stripping the redundant canes out of the trellising system. These then have to be mulched (there are now ways of stripping using a machine which also mulches at the same time). Finally, the canes that were selected for the following year have to be wrapped onto the fruiting wires and tied down.

Spring

O nce the job of pruning is complete the vines lie dormant until spring when the warmer weather encourages the sap to rise and the vine to reawaken. The first signs of this new life appear with a slightly furry covering over the tiny buds that swell and eventually burst – hence the expression 'budburst'. For sauvignon blanc vines in Marlborough, this is during September though the exact timing is dependent on how warm or cold the weather is just prior.

From September through to the end of November is a worrying period for grape growers as a spring frost can be devastating. The young, tender buds and their shoots are very vulnerable and a severe frost will actually burn them, affecting not only that year's yield but possibly that of the following year as well.

There are a number of measures that can be put in place to prevent this. Though expensive, they are not always guaranteed to work and tend to upset the neighbours. The first is frost fans – large diesel-driven windmills that drive warmer air from above downwards towards the ground. Another method is the employment of helicopters. With the use of lasers positioned in the vineyard, the pilot is directed to the coldest spots where he hovers, pushing the warmer air downwards. A much quieter method is the use of water. Vines can be sprayed using overhead frost protection systems or overhead irrigation. As the water turns into ice it releases heat, so continually applying water to the buds and young leaves and letting it freeze, protects them.

New and replacement vines are also planted in springtime – the tell-tale milk cartons (often used instead of vine guards) protecting the tasty young shoots from rabbits as well as giving them some shelter.

'Bud rubbing' is another springtime job, knocking off the buds that appear down the trunk of the vine.

Summer

Flowering takes place during December and is an important indication of how much fruit the vine will bear. Good weather at this time is important, and while warm winds are fine, a cold southerly can be detrimental. After flowering comes the fruit 'set' when the tiny bunches actually form.

With the growth of the vines comes wire-lifting – not only does this keep the vineyard looking smart and orderly, but it also allows the fruiting zone – where the bunches of grapes form – to be exposed. The rows are then also easily accessed by tractors so that spraying can take place – whether under-vine weed killing or vine treatments, and later by machine-harvesters.

Irrigation is another important part of growing vines in Marlborough – while Old World vineyards don't use irrigation, our soils lack the ability to hold moisture due to their free-draining nature, so water has to be applied frequently.

During February, 'veraison' takes place. The grapes start to soften and change colour turning from green to a more golden hue.

A Waihopai Valley vineyard – grower for Astrolabe

Autumn

n March, everything is geared up for harvest. Picking decisions are based on both the sugar content of the grapes called 'brix' and on the flavours – the physiological ripeness. Sauvignon blanc is a relatively late ripener. This becomes a serious challenge as the longer the grapes are on the vine, the more susceptible to pests and disease they become. For example, wet and warm weather can encourage an outbreak of botrytis. While this is highly desirable in the production of rich, sweet dessert wines, it is not something you want in your fresh, aromatic sauvignon blanc. Yet again, weather plays the key part in determining both quality and quantity of healthy, flavoursome grapes.

Sauvignon blanc is usually harvested during April. Mechanical harvesting is the most common method, ensuring the grapes are picked and taken to the winery in the shortest time. Mechanical harvesters work by shaking the vine at the fruiting zone, collecting only separate grapes – not whole bunches. Another advantage is being able to harvest at night – important for warm areas such as Marlborough because it is desirable to harness the aromas by ensuring the grapes are picked and transported while cool.

Some sauvignon blanc is hand-picked to allow for whole-bunch pressing. This reduces the 'phenolics' – natural compounds in the pulp and skins of the grapes – in the finished wine. Phenolics are natural phenols and polyphenols that have an effect on the colour, taste and texture of the wine. While some phenolic characters are desirable, too much can lead to wines that taste and feel very hard and coarse.

Stainless steel tanks
of sauvignon blanc
juice at Wither Hills

The Winery

One of the greatest innovations in the wine industry, one that ensures wine lovers can enjoy the wine exactly as the winemaker intended, is the screw cap closure. These closures preserve every aspect of the wine as they are non-porous and form a 100 per cent seal. Cork, on the other hand, offers huge variability – bottles of wine from the same vintage can vary significantly, depending on the quality of the cork used. Random oxidation is a serious fault and is due to poor cork quality, as well as what is called 'scalping' of aroma and flavour. In addition to these challenges, cork bark is prone to a certain type of fungus that releases TCA (2,4,6-trichloroanisole), as a by-product. It is this TCA that permeates the cork, which in turn permeates the wine with its damp, musty smell and flavour. After all those years of nurturing the vineyard and its precious grapes through to the finished wine, for it to be bought and lovingly stored perhaps for years, the disappointment of opening it up with great anticipation and finding it ruined by the cork is jaw-droppingly disappointing.

To help preserve the aromatics, sauvignon blanc grapes tend to be picked in the cool of the early morning often around four o'clock, to the delight of all concerned. The vast majority of Marlborough sauvignon blanc is harvested by machine – this does not adversely affect the quality, but rather allows the grapes to be picked and taken to the winery in the shortest time.

On arrival at the winery the grapes are tipped into a crusher-destemmer that crushes the grapes and removes any stems. The juice is chilled and pumped into stainless steel tanks to undergo a cool, temperature-controlled fermentation. After a few rackings (when the wine is taken off the 'lees' – the spent yeasts that fall to the bottom of the tank) the wine is usually fined, filtered and bottled. Some sauvignon blancs are being enjoyed just a few months after being picked!

How to Taste and

1. To open a bottle of screw cap wine, hold the neck of the capsule in your left hand, with the bottle at an angle across your chest, then twist the bottle towards you with your right hand (reverse if you are left-handed). You will hear the 'lugs' break, and then just twist the cap off.

2. Pour some wine – about three centimetres deep – into a glass preferably with a tapered top. As you stop pouring, twist the bottle towards you as you lift it up from the glass to prevent dripping.

3. Pick up the glass by the stem and look at the wine. It should be clear and bright.

4. Still holding the stem, swirl the wine around in the glass – this creates more surface area helping to release the wine's aroma and because of the tapered shape of the glass, the aroma remains 'trapped' rather than dissipating immediately.

5. Stick your nose in and sniff. First impressions count! What does it smell of? Swirl and sniff several times to help you determine what aromas there are.

6. Take a mouthful and slosh it around as if it is mouthwash. This gets the wine to all the different receptors in your mouth giving you different indications. The tip of your tongue will detect sweetness; the sides to the front pick up saltiness; the sides to the back, sourness; and right at the back is where you will detect any bitterness. Acidity is felt along the gums giving you that 'mouth-watering' sensation. Tannin, found mainly in red wines is the drying effect you can feel – almost like having furry teeth.

Enjoy

7. Suck in some air over your palate – go on, make that slurping sound, just like when sipping hot soup from a mug. This helps aerate the wine and encourage the flavours to reveal themselves.

8. When you swallow the wine, what impression are you left with? What's the finish like? Can you still taste the flavours of the wine or just feel the physical sensations? A good quality wine will have good length of flavour.

9. Repeat numbers 4 to 7 again to double-check your findings.

10. If you liked the wine, pour a few more centimetres, sit back and enjoy.

This is just a suggestion for when you are trying a new wine – not something you do with every mouthful!

Storage

If a bottle of wine is sealed with a screw cap you can store it standing up or lying down. If it has a cork you need to keep it lying down so that the cork stays covered by the wine in the bottle, preventing it from drying out and letting air in – one of the ways a wine can become oxidised.

Wine needs to be kept at a constant temperature – preferably cool. It also likes being kept away from bright light and vibration.

Cellaring

Cellaring sauvignon blanc is a matter of taste. As a rule of thumb, the vast majority of these wines are made with early enjoyment in mind – within 12 to 18 months of the vintage. The naturally fruit-driven, pungent styles mellow with extra time in the bottle, sometimes resulting in relatively flat wines, or with 'tinned asparagus' characters. However, there are some styles, particularly those that have more mineral tones, which can be rewarding after more time in the bottle – from two to four years and even longer for some.

Glasses

To fully enjoy sauvignon blanc use a decent-sized wine glass that tapers towards the top with an opening that is not too large. You can then swirl the wine to get the full effect of the aromas and when you take a sip, the wine will naturally be directed down your tongue towards the back of your palate. If the glass has a larger opening, when you take a sip the wine is automatically deposited on the sides of your tongue and your gums (because you don't have to tip your head back so far) and these are the areas that pick up acidity. Sauvignon blanc has a naturally high acidity, hence you do not want to accentuate it the minute the wine enters your mouth.

When serving sauvignon blanc, serve it chilled but bear in mind the colder the wine the less aroma and flavour. While it will warm up a little in the glass, the wine doesn't need to be icy cold in the first place, shutting down all of its character.

There are a number of styles and a number of descriptors used when tasting and enjoying this wine style. As a generalisation, the wines tend to be fresh and zesty with an aroma that hits you at 40 paces, one sniff and the taste buds are tingling with anticipation. The array of pungent flavours can include ripe and juicy with tropical fruits or follow a more herbaceous style with chopped capsicum, citrus and grassy overtones.

Allan Scott Family Winemakers

www.allanscott.com

The team at Allan Scott hold two elements close to their hearts – family and experience. The family operate the business with Allan at the helm and his wife, Cathy alongside. Daughter Sara is the viticulturist, son Josh is the winemaker while older daughter Victoria handles the marketing.

With the company vineyards close to the winery in Jacksons Road, Sara and Josh have complete control when it comes to selecting fruit for the three different sauvignon blancs produced under the Allan Scott label. The flagship wine is the Allan Scott Marlborough Sauvignon Blanc, a blend of several vineyards, while the two single-vineyard wines are drawn from the Millstone organic vineyard and

the Moorlands vineyard.

A visit to the Allan Scott winery offers the temptations of the welcoming Twelve Trees Restaurant and a well-stocked cellar door showcasing arts and crafts as well as the family's wines.

**ALLAN SCOTT
THE MOORLANDS
MARLBOROUGH
SAUVIGNON BLANC**
A top-line wine offering grapefruit and tangerine on the nose with a smooth, weighty texture across the palate. Ripe fruit characters with tropical hints are balanced by a refreshing acidity on the finish.

ARA

www.winegrowersofara.co.nz

Ara is a special piece of land – situated just to the west of the township of Renwick – and to the south of State Highway 63 leading towards the South Island's West Coast. The word 'Ara' has significant meaning. In Maori, Ara means 'pathway', while to the Romans it signified a 'shrine'. Ara's philosophy is one of new and old coming together to create a blend of tradition and innovation based on the unique geological feature that is the Ara land. The company's viticultural techniques are based on the Old World

philosophies of high vine density and low yield, therefore translating the vineyard's purest characters into the finished wine. The winemaking culture is one of non-intervention – as much as possible allowing the wine to display the vineyard's characteristics with minimal winemaking influence.

Considerably more than just another Marlborough wine producer, Ara is a culture in itself. It is radical in today's New World wines, particularly with the European approach of close vine planting and low yields. And yet this is what Ara is about. This is what makes the wines and the overall approach so different and so compelling. With the proof in the wine, many are quick to benchmark the styles against the finest sauvignon blancs from France, which are far more about a sense of place than merely the primary fruit characters. Descriptors such as sinuous, taut, subtle, satisfying and complex are often associated with these wines.

Ara makes a number of distinct ranges, among them the Select Blocks, Pathway and Single Estate each of them including a sauvignon blanc. With a backbone of fine acidity, mineral tones and a more restrained fruit style, these wines flourish over two to five years delivering complexity and enjoyment in an understated fashion. Like their French counterparts, these wines are ideal food partners as they underline and enhance rather than compete and overpower. The delicate flavours of shellfish and seafood, or lightly-dressed salads are perfect as are any number of subtle dishes. Equally these wines make perfect aperitifs.

ARA Select Blocks Sauvignon Blanc is the company's premium-level wine. It is a blend of grapes from carefully selected areas of the vineyard, therefore delivering the most complete expression of Ara's land with the aim of delivering absolute consistency year on year in terms of style, flavour and balance.

ARA Single Estate Sauvignon Blanc is a slightly more fruit-forward style also created from a blend of grapes. The resulting wine offers a true expression of the land while combining the renowned Marlborough vivaciousness with the elegance and texture for which Ara is fast becoming internationally recognised.

While the practises at Ara draw on traditional, long-established methods, the company's branding is contemporary. A fresh approach to wine labelling attracts the wine lover to the story that offers a unique point of difference on today's cluttered wine shelves.

ARA sauvignon blancs are some of the few Marlborough styles that will age gracefully, taking on a slightly more mellow, seamless range of flavours as the wines gently evolve.

ARA SELECT BLOCKS SAUVIGNON BLANC
Enticing aromas of stone fruit and juicy grapefruit are also echoed on the palate. The texture is weighty and contributes to the length of flavour, while a fresh acidity provides the perfect balance.

ARA SINGLE ESTATE SAUVIGNON BLANC
Elderflower, lemon zest and good old-fashioned lemon and barley on the nose lead to a textural palate with a refreshing acidity and intense, concentrated orchard fruits. Well-balanced with some mineral complexities on the finish.

Oysters Three Ways
with: Basil Oil Dressing; Salmon Caviar; & Au Natural

 WINE MATCH
ARA Single Estate Sauvignon Blanc

Basil Oil Dressing:
1 cup tightly-packed basil leaves
½ cup extra virgin olive oil
3 tablespoons lemon juice
salt and white pepper to taste
1 chorizo sausage
1 teaspoon olive oil, extra

24 oysters
8 large basil leaves
4-5 tablespoons salmon caviar
1-2 tablespoons mirin
1 lemon

Blanch the basil briefly in boiling water, until limp. Drain and pat dry. Place with a ¼ cup of olive oil in a small blender. Process, until smooth. Strain.

Whisk the strained oil together with the lemon juice and seasonings. Set aside.

Skin the chorizo. Dice. Briefly fry in the remaining olive oil, until crisp. Drain and pat dry.

To serve, place the oysters in shells or individual serving dishes. Place a basil leaf in eight of the shells or dishes. Top each with an oyster, a little basil oil dressing and the chorizo. Top eight more oysters with a little mirin and the salmon caviar. Top the remaining oysters with a squeeze of lemon juice.

SERVES 4 AS A NIBBLE.

A

Astrolabe

www.astrolabewines.co.nz

Astrolabe is the epitome of excellent Marlborough sauvignon blanc. Director and winemaker Simon Waghorn works his own special magic with this grape variety revealing both its true characteristics and regional identity in every bottle.

Established in 1996, the grapes are sourced from 12 carefully chosen vineyards across the Marlborough region as well as Astrolabe's own holdings at Grovetown and the lower Waihopai Valley. Marlborough sauvignon blanc constitutes 80 per cent of the overall Astrolabe production with several different wines in the portfolio including Taihoa Single Vineyard from the Kekerengu Coast, Awatere Valley and the blended Marlborough Province label.

The Kekerengu and Awatere Sauvignon Blancs are part of Astrolabe's Valleys range reflecting Marlborough's fast-emerging subregions. These wines highlight the attributes of individual districts translating their characteristics through to the finished wines.

Kekerengu Sauvignon Blanc from the southern part of the Marlborough region towards Kaikoura is a slightly softer version. The dramatic eastern coast with its crashing waves and rocky outcrops belies the peaceful vineyards from which this wine was crafted. This area boasts the longest growing season, often two weeks behind the other subregions. With free-draining stony, silty loam over limestone, the flinty aromas together with citrus zest and almost an almost salty tang on the palate certainly pay homage to its origins.

ASTROLABE AWATERE VALLEY SAUVIGNON BLANC
This well-structured wine offers a sinuous combination of lime juice and a flinty minerality with that 'after the rain' fresh aroma. Citrusy and herbaceous, dry yet offering ripe nectarine and white peach characters, this complex wine is both delicious and rewarding.

A

Simon is one of the only few winemakers currently exploiting this region and both the Astrolabe team and their customers love the results.

Astrolabe Marlborough Sauvignon Blanc is made from grapes grown in a number of vineyards. Simon carefully selects different blocks to reflect the complexity and diversity of the Marlborough region. From the clay-based soils of the Awatere to the bonier, friable soils of the Wairau, the end result is a wine that combines ripe fruit characters with more earthy, almost savoury tones.

ASTROLABE KEKERENGU COAST SAUVIGNON BLANC
The aromas of this wine are reminiscent of lemon meringue pie – fresh and citrusy with a hint of biscuit. Passionfruit is also apparent along with a more gentle acidity and a hint of warmed earth. This wine has a rewarding texture and though dry, is fleshy and supple giving it great balance.

ASTROLABE MARLBOROUGH SAUVIGNON BLANC
Inviting, lifted, pronounced nose with tempting mineral characters, fresh herbs and white peach. This dry wine has an intense and powerful, fruity mid-palate and lots of fleshy, rich and ripe flavours. With a lovely fresh acidity and great length, this wine is a stunner.

Avocado, Scallop & Coriander Salad

WINE MATCH
Astrolabe Marlborough Sauvignon Blanc

Dressing:
¼ cup lime juice
1 teaspoon chopped chilli
¼ cup extra virgin olive oil
½ teaspoon sugar

25g butter
2 cloves garlic, crushed
24 scallops
1 large avocado
1 small shallot, sliced
½ cup packed coriander sprigs

To make the dressing, process the ingredients in a blender, until smooth.

Melt the butter in a medium-sized pan. Add the garlic and scallops. Sauté on medium heat for about 1 minute each side, until cooked. Remove and cool.

Peel, stone and slice the avocado.

Arrange the scallops, avocado, shallot and coriander on a platter and season with salt and pepper. Drizzle the dressing over the salad. **SERVES 4 AS A STARTER OR 2 AS A MAIN.**

A

Auntsfield's Luc Cowley (winemaker) and Ben Cowley (viticulturist)

Auntsfield Estate

www.auntsfield.co.nz

Auntsfield is a family affair with Graeme and Linda Cowley joined by their sons Luc and Ben as winemaker and viticulturist respectively. When the family bought the estate they had no idea it was once Marlborough's first vineyard. Beginning in 1873, David Herd produced wine for 50 years before returning the land to a sheep farm. The Cowleys pay significant respect to the heritage of their land, making wines that are representative of the classic Marlborough style but with a firm nod to the land they have nurtured just as David Herd did all those years ago.

Nestled among the lower slopes of the southern hills of Marlborough's Wairau Valley, Auntsfield Estate sits on an elevated site with views over the valley and to the Pacific Ocean. The diverse range of soil types from glacial, riverbed and volcanic influences together with the pocketed meso-climates give a complexity and minerality to the wines highlighting their sense of place. This is further endorsed by the family's winemaking philosophy 'To produce wine of uncompromised quality from grapes grown at our family vineyard, Auntsfield Estate.'

Winemaker Luc talks about the importance of ensuring balance when making top quality wines and believes that with today's technology and expertise, quality should be a given. As a result, his mission is 'To make exciting wines of individuality; wines with personality. I strive for the wines I make to be complex yet varietal and to reflect the terroir without being bound by it.'

As Ben goes about his work in the vineyard, he often thinks about David Herd: 'Everywhere he trod, I now tread. Everything he experienced with weather and conditions, I now experience.' Though Ben acknowledges his 4WD motorbike probably makes life easier than working with horses back in David's time, he has a healthy respect for the land and this is demonstrated in the Auntsfield wines. 'There is nothing better at the end of a hard day's work than sitting down and experiencing an Auntsfield wine that expresses who and what we are. A true sense of place.'

AUNTSFIELD SAUVIGNON BLANC

Lifted, fleshy, ripe style of sauvignon blanc with succulent passionfruit, lime and apple flavours. Balanced and well structured, with an underlying minerality and weighty texture, this is a delicious wine that can complement some very flavoursome dishes.

Grilled Salmon with Pomegranate Glaze

WINE MATCH
Auntsfield Sauvignon Blanc 2010

½ cup pomegranate syrup or molasses
2 tablespoons orange juice
1 tablespoon soy sauce
1 tablespoon Dijon-style mustard
8 salmon loins or 600g salmon fillets

Combine the pomegranate syrup, orange juice, soy sauce and mustard. Brush about half over the skinless sides of the salmon. Marinate in the refrigerator for 10-20 minutes.

Preheat the grill or a ridged frying pan to medium heat. Cook the salmon on medium-low, about 2-4 minutes each side depending on the thickness. Baste once during cooking with the reserved sauce.

Great served with a rocket or watercress salad and potato rosti.
SERVES 4.

Barking Hedge

www.crightonestate.co.nz

Barking Hedge comes from Crighton Estate, a family-owned 20-hectare vineyard that runs alongside State Highway 63 just outside the township of Renwick. Named after the antics of dog Jazmine who loves to bark at hedgehogs, the wine was first produced in 2007 when the family decided to launch their own label instead of continuing to grow for other local producers.

Crighton Estate is making a concerted effort to reduce the amount of chemical sprays used in the vineyard by continuous soil testing and applying only what is required. In addition, the team cultivates between the rows and plants wild flowers to attract the bees.

The company's grape-growing attitude is to ensure viticultural management that complements their philosophy of growing wine not grapes and ensuring quality not quantity. Consultant winemaker Steve Bird makes the Barking Hedge wines for the Crightons, while they market them both locally and overseas to the USA, UK, Canada, Europe and Australia.

BARKING HEDGE SAUVIGNON BLANC
A subtle, slightly more rounded version of sauvignon blanc with citrus and apple flavours together with a refreshing acidity. A lovely pre-dinner drink with nibbles, cheese and biscuits.

B

Bird Sauvignon Blanc

www.birdwines.com

Steve Bird has been making wines for over 30 years, starting pretty much straight from school, though he did complete a degree in wine science at Roseworthy Agricultural College in South Australia.

Steve established Bird Winery and Vineyards in 2006 after working for a number of high profile wine producers and establishing Thornbury wines, which was later purchased by a larger organisation. As well as making wine for his own label, he consults to a number of other producers helping them to showcase their vineyard in each bottle of wine.

Steve's philosophy dictates that the wine should be a pure expression of the vineyard, vintage and variety. His goal is to take the best fruit and guide it through the winery in a way that allows the natural characters of the variety to shine. He explains, 'The wines must exhibit purity of varietal characters. They must be aromatic, flavoursome and textural, but above all they must be balanced and harmonious.'

Grapes for Bird Sauvignon Blanc 2010 came from the Old Schoolhouse Vineyard in Marlborough's Omaka Valley. The vineyard was named after the historic schoolhouse built in 1896 which still stands in the vineyard today. The soils are an ideal combination of free-draining alluvial shingle with friable clay loam on top.

Based in Tauranga but passionate about Marlborough and its wines, Steve has focussed heavily on the export markets with considerable success. Bird Sauvignon Blanc can now be enjoyed in a dozen or more countries with further markets on the cards.

BIRD SAUVIGNON BLANC
A subtle nose yet showing ripe, succulent orchard fruits with a hint of citrus. Quite a fleshy style with a lovely balance of fresh acidity and an array of lingering flavours. A great style as an aperitif or ideal with lighter dishes such as fresh salads, seafood and tomato-based sauces.

Mussels in a Tomato & Saffron Sauce

WINE MATCH
Bird Sauvignon Blanc

24 medium mussels
¼ cup sauvignon blanc
2 tablespoons olive oil
2 shallots, diced
400g can Italian tomatoes in juice, chopped
¼ teaspoon saffron threads
flaky sea salt and freshly ground black pepper to taste
fresh herbs to garnish

Scrub the mussels under cold running water. Using scissors, trim the beards.

Heat the wine in a large saucepan. Add the mussels. Cover and steam until the mussels open. Shake occasionally. Discard any that don't open. Strain the wine and reserve.

Heat the oil in the saucepan. Add the shallots and sauté for 1 minute on low heat. Add the tomatoes, saffron and strained wine. Simmer for about 2 minutes. Season. Add the mussels and heat through. Garnish. **SERVES 2 AS A MAIN OR 4 AS A STARTER.**

B

Brancott Estate vineyard
in the Wairau Valley

B

Brancott Estate

www.brancottestate.com

Brancott Estate's Letter Series is the company's leading premium varietal range with each wine named in honour of its vineyard. All Letter Series wines are given bottle ageing appropriate to the varietal prior to release, thereby ensuring optimal drinking.

Brancott Estate is named after the Brancott vineyard, where Frank Yukich, founder of Montana (as the company was formerly known) planted the region's first sauvignon blanc vines in the mid-1970s. The release of the first vintage four years later was the beginning of a phenomenon that not only placed New Zealand firmly on the international map, but also formed the basis for the New Zealand wine industry's world-wide reputation. Within 10 years of this first vintage, Montana's Marlborough Sauvignon Blanc had won the prestigious Marquis de Goulaine Trophy for Best Sauvignon Blanc at the International Wine and Spirits Competition in London – the first of many trophies for Marlborough sauvignon blanc.

Brancott vineyard is on the southern side of the Wairau Valley and is characterised by older, more structural soils with a higher clay content. Formed from glacial outwash and wind-blown loess, they are still free-draining, but have a much higher nutrient content than those on the northern side of the valley. The resulting sauvignon blanc wines are flavoursome, textural and have a vibrant, greener edge.

The winemaking team at Brancott, which – in 2009 – celebrated the company's 30th vintage, has almost 100 years of experience between them, ensuring consumers receive a reliable, consistently high-quality wine as they strive to deliver excellence with every vintage. Sustainability is high on the list with the company a founding member of New Zealand's original sustainable winegrowing initiative established in 1995.

Brancott vineyard is also home to the iconic Marlborough Food and Wine Festival held in February every year. Eight thousand people come to enjoy a great day of celebrating local wines, local foods and great music with headline acts providing the perfect entertainment. The new cellar door overlooking the Brancott vineyard is the ideal place to enjoy lunch with a view. Daily tours are offered showcasing New Zealand's native falcons protecting the vines from bird pests.

BRANCOTT 'B' MARLBOROUGH SAUVIGNON BLANC
A richer style of sauvignon with an almost creamy character on the nose, together with fresh, underlying orchard fruits. Rounded and fleshy with a smooth texture, this wine has lovely concentrated ripe fruits and a mineral finish.

Almond-crusted Fish

WINE MATCH
Brancott 'B' Marlborough Sauvignon Blanc

2 skinned and boned white fish fillets, about 150g each

Crust:
3 tablespoons sliced almonds
25g softened butter
2 tablespoons fine dry breadcrumbs
1 tablespoon each: finely grated Parmesan cheese,
    finely chopped flat-leaf parsley
1 teaspoon finely grated lemon peel
salt and freshly ground black pepper to taste

1 lemon, cut into wedges

Preheat the oven to 220°C.

Place the fish in a lightly oiled baking pan. Combine the ingredients for the crust. Pat evenly over the fish.

Bake for 6-8 minutes – depending on thickness.

Great topped with a squeeze of lemon juice. **SERVES 2.**

Catalina Sounds'
Serendipity vineyard

Catalina Sounds

www.catalinasounds.co.nz

Catalina Sounds, named after the majestic Catalina flying boats that played such a vital role across the South Pacific during and after World War II, produce wines from their vineyard high on a ridge in the Waihopai Valley. The site is at an elevation of 182.8 metres (600 feet) and enjoys hot summers and very cold winters; ideal conditions for growing cool-climate varieties such as sauvignon blanc.

Marlborough interested winemaker, Nina Stocker from her days of working in a bar while at university. She was often asked by customers for a Marlborough 'savvy' so she decided to look into this popular wine style. When she found that Marlborough offered the ability to produce a diverse range of wine styles with its cool climate, plenty of sunshine and interesting subregions (as well as the spectacular surroundings) she decided she wanted to live and work there.

Since the first release of sauvignon blanc in 2005, Catalina Sounds winemaking philosophy has focused on the fruit – sourcing the best grapes from Marlborough's different subregions to blend with grapes from their own vineyard. Each parcel is kept separate throughout the winemaking process until blending when Nina makes her decisions based on the expression shown in each wine. Nina's personal mantra is to produce sauvignon blanc that has elegance, fruit intensity, complexity and balance. The quality of the vineyards and fruit is her focus and she is adamant that her role as winemaker is at best secondary to the role of the vineyards in producing great wines. 'I prefer the fruit to express itself. I love wines that are food-friendly, not over the top. Subtle, well-balanced, elegant wines are what I like to drink and what I like to make.'

Nina and her team were delighted when they received recognition for their efforts when the 2009 Catalina Sounds Marlborough Sauvignon Blanc rose to international acclaim winning the Champion Sauvignon Blanc Trophy at the 2009 Air New Zealand Wine Awards.

From the 2010 vintage onwards all Catalina Sounds wines carry the Sustainable Wine Growers New Zealand (SWNZ) accreditation.

CATALINA SOUNDS SAUVIGNON BLANC
Lifted and fresh with grassy, herbaceous aromas followed by a balanced array of flavours including lemon zest, green apples and fresh basil. Mineral undertones come through giving this wine an almost savoury hint on the finish.

Asparagus Caesar Salad

WINE MATCH
Catalina Sounds Sauvignon Blanc

2 slices brown bread
2 tablespoons garlic-infused rice bran oil
250g asparagus
4 cups torn cos lettuce leaves
1 cup cherry tomatoes, halved
½-¾ cup good Caesar salad dressing
½ cup finely grated parmesan cheese

Preheat the oven to 200°C.

Cut the bread into 1cm cubes. Toss with the rice bran oil. Place in a roasting pan. Bake for about 10 minutes, until crisp and golden, stirring once or twice during cooking. Drain on paper towels.

Trim the asparagus – peel any thick ends with a potato peeler. Steam or blanch quickly in boiling water until crisp-tender. Drain and refresh in icy water. Pat dry.

In a large bowl, combine the cos lettuce, asparagus, cherry tomatoes and bread croutons. Toss with a little of the dressing. Sprinkle with the parmesan and serve immediately. **SERVES 3-4.**

Clark Estate

www.clarkestate.co.nz

The vision at Clark Estate, through viticulturist and winemaker Simon Clark and his sister Sarah, is to make a single-vineyard Awatere Valley sauvignon blanc that is complex and fruit driven and ages well. The team strives to create a well-balanced wine with intricate layers of ripe, tropical characters contrasted with fresh herbaceous aromas. These characteristics are encouraged in the vineyard with the development of a number of blocks based on different soils. These are all managed individually to enhance the separate identities, resulting in ripe fruit of varying flavour profiles. These parcels are kept separate in the winery and following fermentation, some lees aging adds complexity and texture before blending the various blocks together.

Through intense canopy management Simon is able to pick on separate dates to maximise fruit maturity and therefore the flavours.

CLARK ESTATE SINGLE VINEYARD SAUVIGNON BLANC
Lifted gooseberry and freshly chopped capsicum aromas followed by delicious sweet, ripe fruit and a lovely tangy acidity give the wine good structure. Long and concentrated with a mineral tone on the finish, this is a well made, polished wine.

Clayfork Vineyard

www.catalinasounds.co.nz

Located in the Waihopai Valley this vineyard comprises four blocks of sauvignon blanc, all with slightly different characteristics. The focus for this small quantity, single-vineyard wine is on allowing the site to express itself. Each block is harvested individually and on several different dates to ensure optimal ripeness and balance.

Winemaker Alan Peter-Oswald's various techniques include some whole-bunch pressing, barrel fermentation in French oak and lees contact for up to seven months to develop a textural and slightly more austere style of wine that matches well with food and has good ageing potential.

Alan's philosophy is for sauvignon blanc to be an expression of the vineyards and sub-regions in which the grapes were grown, allowing each parcel of fruit to show its own unique personality.

CLAYFORK VINEYARD WAIHOPAI RIDGE SAUVIGNON BLANC
This wine is very different as it has had some oak influence and time on yeast lees. It's rich, creamy texture offers ripe, tropical fruit. Balanced by a fresh acidity, it is ideal with dishes such as chicken, creamy, herbed pasta and salads.

Cloudy Bay

www.cloudybay.co.nz

This famous winery takes its name from the bay at the most eastern point of the Wairau Valley where the Wairua River flows into the Cook Strait. It was named Cloudy Bay by Captain Cook on his voyage to New Zealand in 1770.

When it comes to Cloudy Bay Sauvignon Blanc, everyone can picture the wine's famous label featuring the misty peaks of the Richmond Ranges. This iconic wine was the catalyst in the creation of the significant force that Marlborough sauvignon blanc has become, blazing a trail for the aromatic, pungent, purity of style that the region is now so famous for.

Cloudy Bay was established in 1985 by David Hohnen who also established Western Australia's Cape Mentelle winery. Converted from sheep and cattle land, the first Cloudy Bay vineyard, the 'Home Block' on Jacksons Road, was planted in 1986. However, with the arrival of phylloxera in the region, it had to be replanted with resistant rootstocks in 1992. The company draws grapes from four company sites in Renwick, the Brancott Valley, Rapaura and Omaka as well as from a select number of growers across the region.

Owned by luxury goods giant, Louis Vuitton Moët Hennessy, Cloudy Bay is part of a portfolio that offers some of the world's finest brands – a fitting position given the wine's history and reputation.

Cloudy Bay's cellar door maintains a local feel and is a popular destination for wine lovers and offers a welcoming taste of the company's wines, including several only available on-site.

Exported to more than 30 destinations around the world Cloudy Bay, once sold only on allocation, is now available to meet the strong global demand.

CLOUDY BAY SAUVIGNON BLANC

An elegant translation of sauvignon blanc with fresh lime, a touch of tropical fruit and clean, zesty acidity. A favourite of many over the years, this style hints of classic Marlborough while retaining a sense of self. Good length with a touch of 'wet stones' on the finish.

Gazpacho

 WINE MATCH
Cloudy Bay Sauvignon Blanc

2 x 400g cans tomatoes in juice, roughly chopped
4 cloves garlic
1 large red pepper (capsicum), chopped
½ cup basil leaves
¼ cup extra virgin olive oil
2 tablespoons red wine vinegar
1 cup each: stale French bread cubes, chilled tomato juice

Topping:
1 each: red pepper (capsicum), onion, tomato
1 cup toasted bread croûtons
6 basil leaves
freshly ground salt and pepper to taste

Place the tomatoes and juice, garlic, red pepper, basil, olive oil, vinegar and bread cubes in a bowl and refrigerate for several hours or overnight. Purée in a food processor. Sieve if preferred. Add enough tomato juice to create a soup consistency. Chill.

Seed the red pepper and dice. Dice the onion and tomato. Serve on top of the soup with the croûtons, basil, salt and pepper. **SERVES 6.**

Cloudy Bay's Red Shed
vineyard on Conders
Bend Road

Cloudy Bay Te Koko

www.cloudybay.co.nz

Beginning with trials back in 1991, Te Koko is now, some 20 years later, a much-celebrated wine, revered by both winemakers and wine lovers worldwide. The trials involved using indigenous yeasts – in other words yeasts that are naturally present in the winery rather than inoculating the wine with cultured yeast. This meant trusting the wine to nature. Even at first, when the wine wasn't quite perfect, the winemakers had great faith. This certainly paid off, and after time in oak and three years for the individual parcels of fruit to blend seamlessly, the wine showed an individuality that was both exciting and rewarding.

Te Koko grapes come from the same vineyards as the celebrated Cloudy Bay Sauvignon Blanc though the parcels are identified at harvest and kept separate. Made in only small quantities, demand for this wine always exceeds supply giving it a wonderful cult appeal. Chefs adore the challenge of creating dishes to match Te Koko – its rich texture and flavours giving it a multi-dimensional appeal. Being quite weighty, Te Koko works well with slightly heavier dishes whereas the more traditional style of Marlborough sauvignon blanc demands lighter, fresher flavours.

The name Te Koko comes from Maori legend and the great warrior Kupe. As the story goes, Kupe in his waka (Maori canoe) pursued a huge octopus across the Pacific, finally catching and killing it in the Marlborough Sounds. It was said that the octopus thrashing around created the Sounds themselves. While Kupe was exploring this new land, he dredged for oysters using a scoop. Local Maori named the bay Te Koko-o-Kupe – or 'Kupe's scoop', part of what we know today as Cloudy Bay, at the north-east of New Zealand's South Island. The Te Koko label shows a stylised pattern reflecting the wake of Kupe's canoe and paying homage to the wine's Maori influences.

CLOUDY BAY TE KOKO
Rich aromas of cashew nut and piercing passionfruit together with creamy, fresh vanilla combine to give an exciting nose. This leads to a multi-layered palate with citrus, tropical fruit and a stunning, rich mouth-feel. A full-bodied wine that is intensely satisfying – perfect on release or to cellar for some years.

Veal with Tarragon

WINE MATCH
Cloudy Bay Te Koko

1kg veal leg steak, cubed
salt and pepper to taste
flour for dusting
2 tablespoons olive oil
4 large sprigs fresh French tarragon
½ cup each: sauvignon blanc, good quality beef stock, cream

Preheat the oven to 160°C.

Dust the cubed veal with seasoned flour. Heat the oil in a non-stick frying pan. Sauté the veal, until lightly coloured on all sides. Place in a casserole.

Add one sprig of tarragon and the sauvignon blanc to the frying pan. Bring to the boil, stirring continuously. Add the stock then pour into the casserole.

Cover and cook in the oven for 2 hours or until very tender. Add the cream and remaining tarragon and cook for a further 10 minutes.

Excellent served with potato mash or fettuccine and lightly dusted with paprika. **SERVES 6-8.**

The Richmond Range forms a picturesque backdrop to Dog Point's hillside vineyards

D

Dog Point

www.dogpoint.co.nz

The name Dog Point dates from the earliest European settlement of Marlborough and the introduction of sheep. Dogs belonging to the shepherds sometimes became lost or wandered off and eventually bred into a marauding pack that attacked local flocks. Their home was a tussock and scrub covered hill overlooking the Wairau Plains, named Dog Point by the early settlers.

While it might have made sense to have a dog on the wine label, the singular cabbage tree, or Ti Kouka in Maori, makes a stark yet stylish statement. Common in the Dog Point area, the cabbage tree's remarkable natural qualities and strong geographical identity have a synergy with the Dog Point wines that are a natural expression of the land from which they are created. The distinctive label was iconic right from the outset.

Dog Point Vineyard is owned and managed by highly-respected husband and wife teams, Ivan and Margaret Sutherland and James and Wendy Healy. Famed for gathering a cult following almost prior to the release of the first vintage in 2002, Ivan and James specialise in producing outstanding wines that are the epitome of both the vineyard and winemakers' skill. The wines are made from grapes sourced from selected vineyard plantings dating back to the late 1970s. These older well-established vines are situated on free-draining, silty, clay loams and supplemented with fruit from closely planted hillside vines with a clay loam influence.

As well as Dog Point Sauvignon Blanc, Ivan and James also make Section 94 which refers to a sauvignon blanc made solely from a particular vineyard block. The wine receives extended lees aging in old French oak casks to add complexity and depth, but perhaps most importantly a weighty, layered texture. It's this texture together with the array of intense flavours that has propelled this wine to fame.

Dog Point Vineyard Sauvignon Blanc is everything you would expect in a classical Marlborough sauvignon, only more intense, more complex and more textural. A satisfying and rewarding wine that can only come from those with great fruit, extensive experience and a deep knowledge of their craft.

DOG POINT SAUVIGNON BLANC
The nose on this wine shows the 'wild ferment' characters – fresh thyme, elderflower, passionfruit and lemon zest. Concentrated, full-bodied and with a richness and depth of flavour that gives a wonderful sense of satisfaction. Complex and beautifully balanced.

Flounder Rolls with Seaweed Sauce

WINE MATCH
Dog Point Sauvignon Blanc

500g flounder fillets or fish suitable for rolling eg sole, dory
2 cloves garlic, crushed
150g whitebait or crab meat
2 tablespoons karengo fronds or finely chopped nori
50g butter
2 shallots, diced
pinch each: sugar, saffron or turmeric
1 cup sauvignon blanc
1-2 tablespoons capers, rinsed and dried
freshly ground black pepper to taste

Smear the garlic over one side of the fillets. Top with the whitebait or crab meat. Sprinkle with a little of the karengo. Roll up firmly. Secure with toothpicks, if required.

Melt the butter in a large frying pan on medium-low heat.

Gently sauté the rolls in the butter, 2-3 minutes each side. Remove from the pan and keep warm.

Add the shallots to the pan. Sauté for 1-2 minutes. Add the sugar, saffron or turmeric and wine. Stir well then strain. Boil rapidly until reduced. Add the capers, pepper and remaining karengo. Spoon over the fish and serve. **SERVES 4.**

D

Hand-picking sauvignon
blanc grapes at
Fairbourne Estate

F

Fairbourne Estate

www.fairbourne.co.nz

Fairbourne Estate is a specialist New Zealand wine company owned by husband and wife, Sarah Inkersell and Russell Hooper who aspire 'to produce world-class wine with Marlborough sauvignon blanc.' The reason for focusing solely on this grape variety comes from the couple's extensive experience working with and acknowledging its unique characters. As well as their obvious passion for it, they believe there is more to be discovered about Marlborough sauvignon blanc than is evident in today's widely recognised style.

With its ultra-premium positioning and food-driven style, Fairbourne Sauvignon Blanc graces the tables of many of the world's top restaurants and hotels such as Tetsuya's in Sydney and the Hong Kong Langham. On a recent trip to Asia, Russell was presented with a dish of jellyfish which the chef thought was a particularly good match! The UK is also embracing the wine for its ideal positioning between the majority of Marlborough sauvignon blancs and those from France's Loire Valley, the highly revered Sancerre and Pouilly Fume which tend to retail at far higher prices.

The grapes for Fairbourne are grown on hillside vineyards on the southern side of Marlborough's Wairau Valley. The soils, mainly comprising clay gravels, are less fertile meaning the vines have to work harder to derive the nutrients they require. The result is a lighter crop level and grapes that reflect the true nature of the land. All work in the vineyard is carried out by hand – be it leaf-plucking, shoot-thinning or harvesting. Hand-harvesting minimises skin contact between the juice and grapes, giving Sarah a head start as she crafts the wine into the Fairbourne style.

The other standout part of Fairbourne is the packaging. From the heavy-weight, silky smooth bottle to the embossed label and opulent gift-packaging, this brand just exudes premium.

Fairbourne Estate is a member of The Specialist Winegrowers of New Zealand – a group of six producers who specialise in only one grape variety or one particular style of wine.

FAIRBOURNE SAUVIGNON BLANC
More akin to French sauvignon blanc from the Loire Valley than perhaps the regular Marlborough style, this wine shows a refreshing, steely acidity and a 'wet stone', almost flinty character reflecting the vineyard. Ripe fruit bursts through on the finish leaving a delicious and lasting impression.

Stir-fried Prawns & Snow Peas

WINE MATCH
Fairbourne Estate Sauvignon Blanc

1 egg white
1 tablespoon each: cornflour, sauvignon blanc
500g raw prawns, shelled and deveined
2 teaspoons each: soy sauce, hoisin sauce
1 teaspoon cornflour mixed with 2 tablespoons water
3-4 tablespoons rice bran oil
1 small onion, diced
1 teaspoon each: grated root ginger, crushed garlic
14 snow peas, strings removed, halved
1 lemon, cut into wedges

Combine the egg white, cornflour and wine in a bowl. Add the prawns. Stir to coat. Stand for 30 minutes.

Combine the soy and hoisin sauces. Stir in the cornflour paste.

Heat the oil in a wok. Add the onion and stir-fry until the onion begins to brown. Add the ginger, garlic and snow peas and stir-fry for 1-2 minutes, until the peas are crisp tender. Set aside.

Drain the prawns. Stir-fry until pink, about 2 minutes. Return the snow pea mixture to the pan. Stir the cornflour combo. Mix into the prawns, cooking until thickened. Serve immediately topped with a squeeze of lemon. **SERVES 4 AS A STARTER OR AS PART OF AN ASIAN-STYLE MEAL.**

Fairhall Downs

www.fairhalldowns.co.nz

Fairhall Downs was planted by Ken and Jill Small on eight hectares of land in 1982. In 1996 they decided to make and market their own wine in partnership with their daughter and son-in-law Julie and Stuart Smith. As well as Fairhall Downs Sauvignon Blanc, the company makes Hugo, a truly hand-crafted, 'bells and whistles' sauvignon. Produced using only select parcels of fruit from the family's vineyard in the Brancott Valley, Hugo offers a very different and rewarding interpretation of sauvignon blanc.

The Brancott is one of the region's Southern Valleys and has a dramatic backdrop of the barren Wither Hills while the Fairhall River flows close by. The soils consist of stony, silt loam over clay gravels.

Today, the Small and Smith family land totals almost 32 hectares with 25 hectares of vineyard. This is comprised of just over 16 hectares of sauvignon blanc with the rest split between other varieties.

FAIRHALL DOWNS HUGO SAUVIGNON BLANC
The toasty oak influence is apparent on the nose together with subtle, dried herbs and ripe, tropical fruit. This is a weighty, richer style that gives a luxurious mouth-feel. The flavours are concentrated and rewarding – a complex wine with good cellaring potential.

Forrest

www.forrest.co.nz

Leaving behind careers in molecular biology and medicine respectively, Doctors John and Brigid Forrest returned to Marlborough in 1988 to establish their first vineyard near Renwick, in the heart of the stony Wairau River valley. The company now owns seven and manage a further two vineyards totalling 130 hectares throughout Marlborough's subregions. Vintage 1990 saw the launch of the first Forrest wine and immediate success with a trophy at the national wine awards – a success that has been repeated many times both nationally and internationally over subsequent years.

The Forrest philosophy is one that balances art and science. As John explains, while grape growing and winemaking are exacting sciences, you must have an artistic touch to give the wines 'soul'.

Forrest make one of the few styles of Marlborough sauvignon blanc with the ability to age gracefully. With an emphasis on minerality over fruit, the wine develops a more gentle character, ideal with food as it complements rather than overwhelms the flavours of the dish. Never content with just one version of something, Dr John and his winemaking team will often experiment, coming up with various interpretations of the same grape variety. Sauvignon blanc is no exception with several in the range including The Doctors' Sauvignon Blanc – a lower alcohol, more forward-drinking style.

There are three distinct sauvignon blancs within the Forrest portfolio – Marlborough, promoted as quintessential; the Valleys displaying John's understanding of Marlborough's subregions and their influences; and The Doctors' showcasing the more innovative side of the team's efforts.

Both John and Brigid are heavily involved in the local Marlborough community – from sports facilities and events to the arts and fund-raising for charity.

A warm welcome is assured at the winery's cellar door where there is a large selection of wines to enjoy.

FORREST SAUVIGNON BLANC

Tempting mineral aspects on the nose together with fresh, mouth-watering lime and lemon zest. Lemon flavours continue on the palate together with a fresh leafiness. Succulent and balanced with a flinty finish, this wine is delicious young or will reward cellaring of two to four years.

THE DOCTORS' SAUVIGNON BLANC

Sherbet sweetness on the nose before diving into a luscious palate packed with ripe fruit but balanced with a firm, linear acidity. Seriously drinkable, particularly with the lower alcohol content – it is an ideal aperitif or accompaniment for any number of Asian-inspired dishes.

Framingham
www.framingham.co.nz

Nestling on the outskirts of Renwick alongside Sate Highway 6, which leads to Nelson, is the little haven of Framingham. Walking under the arch into the beautifully manicured gardens sets the scene for an enjoyable cellar door visit.

Framingham is rightly renowned for its aromatic wines, producing a number of highly regarded styles including sauvignon blanc. The very first wine, a riesling, was produced in 1994, though the vineyard was planted back in the early 1980s. The name Framingham comes from the village of Framingham, in Southern Norfolk in the United Kindom. This was the ancestral home of the company's founder, Rex Brooke-Taylor.

The complex Framingham Marlborough Sauvignon Blanc is typically made from a blend of at least a dozen base wines sourced from carefully selected sites in the Wairau Valley including the North Bank, Southern Valleys, Omaka hillsides and the company's own vineyards. The texture of the wine is further enhanced by some barrel fermentation.

FRAMINGHAM SAUVIGNON BLANC
A really pronounced nose, lifted and inviting – very fresh and packed with ripe fruit and a hint of freshly chopped herbs. Lots of layers of flavours – all juicy and succulent. A classic Marlborough sauvignon blanc – well-made and pristine.

Giesen
www.giesen.co.nz

Stamping their name on the wines from the very beginning, the Giesen brothers, Theo, Marcel and Alex have been firmly committed to riding the New Zealand wine wave since the 1980s. With a key focus on making wines that people really want to drink, their styles embrace appeal, ease of enjoyment and value.

Giesen owns 13 vineyards across Marlborough including 300 hectares at Dillons Point. The brothers planted this vineyard in 1993 and today it is their prime site. With so many vineyards under their control (more than 700 hectares), the Giesen team can offer a wide range of components for their wines, giving the winemaking team plenty of choice. This ensures that the house style is maintained while still paying homage to individual vintage traits. Chief winemaker, Andrew Blake has been with the company since 1997 and admits he doesn't have a favourite wine as he enjoys them all.

Andrew shares the brothers' philosophy of producing a range of estate wines with consistency of character, from vintage to vintage.

The Giesen winery is perfect in terms of functionality – an important factor when making consistent, quality wine according to Alex, Marcel and Theo. Their state-of-the-art approach is ideally suited to the purpose of the business – to produce a range of excellent wines. The winery has expanded dramatically since the bare land was purchased in Blenheim in 1999. In 2007 the adjoining land was purchased for expansion and the company now has the ability to process in excess of 7,000 tonnes of grapes and has a tank capacity of 8.5 million litres.

Giesen make three sauvignon blancs – The Estate, The Brothers and The August. The first is appealing and approachable, straightforward and great value. The Brothers takes this same philosophy to the next level with a more intense, individual style. The August is about showcasing style diversity with a sauvignon blanc that can age gracefully after diligent vineyard care and additional winemaking techniques such as oak influence, employed in the winery.

In 2006, the brothers established their own bottling operation which allowed them to double their production capacity. It streamlined the business and was a catalyst for their continued growth in the export markets. The company chose Christchurch as the location – the purpose-built bottling and warehouse facility is just a 30-minute drive to the port of Lyttelton from where the wines are shipped directly to destinations around the world including Australia, Hong Kong, Canada, Japan, Germany, the UK and the USA.

GIESEN MARLBOROUGH SAUVIGNON BLANC
Youthful with pear drop and primary, fresh fruit aromas, this easy, appealing wine smacks of classic Marlborough sauvignon blanc but without being too overpowering. Lovely tropical fruit and herbaceous tones on the finish.

THE BROTHERS SAUVIGNON BLANC
Piercing, lifted nose of pungent herbs and sliced capsicum together with that sweaty element so often sought after by lovers of this style. Concentrated, succulent, a powerful, full-flavoured wine with mineral tones and plenty of expression.

G

Caponata & Goat's Cheese Bruschetta

WINE MATCH
Giesen Marlborough Sauvignon Blanc

Caponata:
1 medium eggplant
3 tablespoons olive oil
1 small onion, diced
1 clove garlic, crushed
2 tablespoons each: tomato paste, water, capers
8 stuffed green olives, diced
2 tablespoons sauvignon blanc
freshly ground black pepper to taste

Brushcetta:
8 slices plain or olive ciabatta
extra virgin olive oil
150g mild goat's cheese diced or crumbled
1 cup baby salad greens

Peel and dice the eggplant. Heat half the oil in a saucepan. Sauté the eggplant, until coloured. Remove. Add the remaining oil to the saucepan. Sauté the onion and garlic, until golden.

Add the combined tomato paste and water. Simmer for 1 minute. Return the eggplant to the pan with the capers and olives. Add the wine. Season, cover and heat gently for 10 minutes, stirring occasionally. Cool, then refrigerate.

Brush the ciabatta with a little oil and grill both sides. Top with the caponata, goat's cheese and salad greens. **SERVES 4.**

Greywacke

www.greywacke.com

After his huge influence as founding winemaker at Cloudy Bay, the release of Kevin Judd's own label was eagerly anticipated. Wine commentators world-wide were hankering to see if his magic would translate elsewhere. It was not a surprise to discover that it did. The first release of Greywacke sold out long before the next vintage. The new label was a bright star in the difficult times of selling wine to an economically-challenged consumer.

Kevin was born in England and grew up in Australia where he studied winemaking at South Australia's Roseworthy College and first made wine at Reynella. He moved to New Zealand in 1983 and worked for Selaks Wines before joining David Hohnen to establish Cloudy Bay, directing the inaugural 25 vintages of what was to become New Zealand's most iconic wine brand.

Kevin's return to hands-on winemaking – from the vineyard through the winery and out into the market – is proving to be a winner. The Greywacke range is primarily based on sauvignon blanc and pinot noir, the sauvignon blanc being produced in two distinctly different styles, namely Greywacke Sauvignon Blanc and Greywacke Wild Sauvignon both of which are explicit examples of this grape variety.

The name Greywacke comes from the sedimentary rock that is the foundation of most of the mountain ranges in New Zealand, it is found almost everywhere – in the rivers, on the beaches and throughout the alluvial soils of the Wairau Plains. These

grey boulders soak up the sun during the long summer days and gently release the warmth through the cooler nights. Kevin registered the name many years ago in the hope of realising his dream of one day – establishing his own solo winemaking venture.

The wines are made by Kevin at Dog Point Winery in the lower Brancott Valley from grapes sourced from mature vineyards within the central Wairau Plains and the Southern Valleys. These prime viticultural sites are cultivated using yield-restricting vineyard management techniques and intense canopy management regimes.

The labels for the Greywacke range are the result of Kevin's other passion, photography. For over two decades his vineyard landscape images, grapevine close-ups and 'Wine Dog' portraits have appeared in countless publications worldwide. His work has also resulted in the publication of several books and an array of highly-coveted, limited edition prints. The Greywacke labels feature signature vineyard images selected from his first book *The Colour of Wine*, digitally converted by Kevin to monochrome and then toned to produce evocative images that represent the wine styles they portray. Kevin's photography can be viewed at www.kevinjudd.co.nz

GREYWACKE SAUVIGNON BLANC
Shiny, piercing nose of concentrated grapefruit, 'wet stones' and a touch of aniseed. Full-bodied with layers of flavours giving a rare complexity that develops further with every sip. Richly textured, ripe yet subtle tropical fruit and a definitive, lingering finish.

GREYWACKE WILD SAUVIGNON
Rich and powerful, the creamy, dynamic nose offers herbs, spice and citrus while the mouth-coating palate gives a great depth of flavour. Fermented using wild rather than cultured yeast, it yields sweetly concentrated, ripe fruit balanced with a firm structure and textural finish.

Hillside vines in the Brancott Valley at Yarrum vineyard grower for Greywacke

Rabbit with Thyme & Olives

WINE MATCH
Greywacke Wild Sauvignon

You may need two rabbits to make up the required weight for this dish.

1.5kg wild rabbit
flour for dusting
3-4 tablespoons olive oil
2 shallots, diced
2 tablespoons each: finely chopped purple sage leaves, thyme leaves
12 pitted black olives
4 cloves garlic, crushed
½ cup each: sauvignon blanc, chicken stock
400g can diced tomatoes
1 vanilla pod
salt and freshly ground black pepper

Preheat the oven to 160°C.

Cut the rabbit into 6 pieces. Dust with flour.

Heat a little of the oil in a heavy casserole suitable for the oven. Sauté the rabbit in batches, until golden. Remove to one side.

Heat a little more oil and sauté the shallots for 1-2 minutes. Then add the herbs, olives and garlic. Return the rabbit to the pan and add the wine, stock and tomatoes. Slit the vanilla pod, scrape out the seeds and add both to the casserole. Season. Cover and cook in the oven for 2½ hours or until the rabbit is tender.

The juices may be thickened with 2 tablespoons of flour mashed together with equal amounts of butter. Gradually stir into the juices and cook for a few minutes, until thick. Excellent served on creamy polenta. **SERVES 6.**

G

Grove Mill

www.grovemill.co.nz

GROVE MILL SAUVIGNON BLANC
With a gentle nose and more subtle array of flavours, this sauvignon blanc is smooth, medium-bodied and easy to enjoy. Orchard fruits fill the palate with a hint of ripe fruit sweetness, balanced by a fresh, citrus acidity.

Herzog

www.herzog.co.nz

One of Marlborough's jewels, Herzog is a Mecca for lovers of fine wine and food. Drawing grapes from their 11-hectare vineyard which surrounds the exclusive fine-dining restaurant and produces just 4000 cases of wine, it is a marvel that Hans Herzog creates so many varietals and all of them outstanding.

Hans' passion lies in the production of Bordeaux-style wines handmade in tiny quantities. Hans nurtures his sauvignon blanc into two styles – a 'Sur Lie' and the 'Grand Duchesse'. The 'Sur Lie' is picked late from very low-yielding grapes and is clearly more reminiscent of white Bordeaux than typical Marlborough sauvignon. The 'Grand Duchesse' is a more exuberant wine showing a fine balance of power and elegance. Hans is fanatical about the quality of his wines and is committed to a non-interventional approach producing authentic, unprocessed and fully natural wines.

HERZOG BARREL-FERMENTED 'SUR LIE' SAUVIGNON BLANC
Some golden yellow colour with this wine and a deliciously inviting nose of crème caramel and melted butter. Silky smooth, weighty and powerful, this Old World interpretation of sauvignon blanc offers ripe fruit and a layered complexity followed by dried herbs on the finish.

Highfield

www.highfield.co.nz

A distinctive statement on the Marlborough skyline with its tall, Tuscan-style tower, Highfield makes another statement with its wines which are designed to be food friendly. Skilled winemaker Al Soper ensures each varietal has time on yeast lees to develop mouth-feel, weight and complexity. Nowhere is this more compelling than with Highfield's Sauvignon Blanc which displays a richness and depth that is uncommon. Another key factor with Highfield's winemaking is that only the free-run juice is used, not that which is extracted from pressing the grapes. This is a costly decision, but one taken to ensure maximum quality and expression while requiring minimum intervention.

The name Highfield originates with the Walsh family from Ireland. They purchased the 365-acre farm in 1935 naming it Highfield after an area near Galway Bay. The family grew crops, grazed stock and bred horses, eventually handing over the reins to son Bill.

Bill was of an entrepreneurial nature and in the mid-70s when he heard that a major New Zealand wine company was considering planting grapes he decided to follow suit. The first planting was two-and-a-half acres of muller thurgau, a medium-sweet German grape variety. Quite by accident, Bill and another local grower discovered some 'rogue' grapes amongst the muller thurgau vines and took cuttings. The plants that subsequently grew proved to be none other than sauvignon blanc and the quality of the wine they produced encouraged the family to make and market this wine under their own label.

Now a global brand, this dynamic and highly successful producer is today owned by Japanese industrialist, Shin Yokoi and UK businessman, Tom Tenuwera. Tom, a wine aficionado, had always loved New Zealand and the warmth of its people – a sentiment shared by his friend Shin. In 1991 they became the new owners of Highfield.

Highfield wines are the perfect accompaniment to the innovative dishes prepared at the restaurant where local produce is a speciality.

HIGHFIELD SAUVIGNON BLANC
This bright and zesty wine offers a passionfruit nose and seductive, creamy texture. Packed with ripe but not overpowering tropical fruit, it is balanced by a refreshing acidity and has great length. Succulent and rewarding.

Classic Seafood Ragout

WINE MATCH
Highfield Sauvignon Blanc

1 cup each: water, sauvignon blanc, milk
1 each: small onion, carrot, sliced
1 each: bay leaf, sprig thyme
250g skinned and boned white fish fillets
6 oysters, scallops or mussels
250g raw prawns, shelled and deveined
25g butter
3 tablespoons flour

Place the water, wine, milk, onion, carrot and herbs in a
saucepan. Simmer for 15 minutes. Strain.

Cut the fish into 3cm pieces. Poach in the strained milk mixture
with the other seafood for 4-5 minutes, until just cooked. Using
a slotted spoon, remove the seafood to one side.

Melt the butter in another saucepan. Stir in the flour. Gradually
whisk in the milk mixture, stirring over low heat, until thick.
Carefully add the seafood and heat through. **SERVES 4 AS
A STARTER.**

Great teamwork from two pastoral industries – sheep graze in Hunter's Omaka vineyard

Hunter's

www.hunters.co.nz

Hunter's, a name synonymous with Marlborough sauvignon blanc from the very early days, planted their initial vineyard in 1979, releasing the first wine just three years later in 1982. In 1986 Hunter's surprised the wine world by winning *The Sunday Times* Vintage Festival in the UK with an oak-aged sauvignon blanc. Irishman, Ernie Hunter who founded the company with his wife Jane, was tragically killed in a car accident in 1987 after just five years of producing his award-winning wines.

Today, under the leadership of Jane Hunter, the company has expanded to six times its original size and increased annual output to 85,000 cases. Jane, together with Gary Duke, chief winemaker for 20 years, create a portfolio of award-winning wines that have won 160 medals and more than 30 trophies to date.

Hunter's goal when making sauvignon blanc is to produce an elegant, well-balanced, flavoursome wine with good length. The desired lifted fruit characters and powerful yet rounded palate, come from blending fruit from various vineyards. The team also view blending as crucial to achieving palate weight, a balanced acidity and an array of intense flavours on the finish. Ernie's catch phrase was 'quality not quantity' and Hunter's production and marketing continues to be based on this philosophy. Gary continues to carefully craft sauvignon blanc with elegance, balance and fruit expression employing a potent blend of old vines, wisdom and experience.

Since 1986, every vintage of Hunter's Sauvignon Blanc has won a gold medal or a trophy at a major wine show. Eighty-five per cent of Hunter's production is exported around the world.

Jane Hunter's success is well recorded. She was awarded an OBE in 1993 for services to the wine industry, appointed a Companion of the New Zealand Order of Merit (CNZM) for services to viticulture in the 2009 New Year's honours list and in 2009, named as a recipient of the annual KEA Trade and Enterprise World Class New Zealand awards, winning the manufacturing category. Jan is a great supporter of the local community and one of the highlights in Marlborough is the annual Hunter's Garden Marlborough held in November each year.

HUNTERS SAUVIGNON BLANC
Fresh and juicy rock melon and chopped garden herbs on the nose then a clean, polished palate with lots of citrus acidity and hints of ripe passionfruit. Classic Marlborough sauvignon blanc with tasty, lingering finish.

Bocconcini & Olive-stuffed Chicken

WINE MATCH
Hunter's Sauvignon Blanc

8 Kalamata olives, pitted and sliced
100g bocconcini or similar, diced
1-2 teaspoons chopped rosemary leaves
freshly ground black pepper to taste
4 small, single, skinned and boned chicken breasts
4-6 slices streaky honey-roasted bacon
2 teaspoons canola oil
¾ cup sauvignon blanc

Preheat the oven to 180°C.

To make the filling, combine the olives, cheese, rosemary and pepper. Pat the chicken dry and season with pepper.

Make a pocket in each chicken breast. Divide the filling between pockets, pressing in well. Wrap a strip of bacon around each breast and secure with cocktail sticks, if required.

Heat the oil in a small, oven-proof pan also suitable for the hob. Brown the chicken, for about 2 minutes each side. Transfer the pan to the middle of the oven and bake until cooked through, about 15 minutes. Remove the chicken to a warm platter.

Add the wine to the pan. Bring to the boil and simmer, stirring, until reduced. Pour over the chicken and serve. **SERVES 4.**

H

Kerner Estate

wwww.kerner.co.nz

KERNER ESTATE SAUVIGNON BLANC
A more reserved style with a soft, rounded and ripe nose. A smooth, easy drinking style more reflective of place than the primary fruit characters of many local sauvignon blancs. Gentle, subtle and a good partner for lighter dishes.

Harvesting at the Lawson's Waihopai Valley vineyard with the 'Dry Hills' in the background

Lawson's Dry Hills

wwww.lawsonsdryhills.co.nz

Ross and Barbara Lawson founded Lawson's Dry Hills in 1992. They had been growing grapes on their Alabama Road vineyard since 1980 before launching their own range of wines. The first vintage was just 15 tonnes and was managed by Ross from an old tin shed that today forms part of the winery cellar door. Lawson's Dry Hills leads the way with aromatic varieties including their excellent sauvignon blanc, winning numerous medals and trophies over the years.

Ross was one of Marlborough's pioneer winemakers and many of the region's wine companies have benefited from his vision and drive – in particular his determination to eradicate cork taint from wine through the New Zealand Screw Cap Wine Seal Initiative of which he was a founding member. Screw caps now seal over 90 per cent of New Zealand's wines and no wine style has benefited more than sauvignon blanc. This was the pinnacle of Ross's influence and of the rich legacy left when he sadly passed away in February 2009.

Lawson's Dry Hills is surrounded by company vineyards and also sources grapes from several growers across the Marlborough region. The sauvignon blanc is typically sourced from seven locations, all within Marlborough's Wairau and Waihopai Valleys, representing a broad cross-section of soil types and microclimates. Five of these vineyards are on the southern side of the Wairau Valley where varying proportions of clay in the soils produce wines with lifted, passionfruit aromas, great concentration and a crisp acidity. The two remaining vineyards are located closer to the coast and contribute an appealing mixture of tropical and herbaceous characters. The timing of picking is crucial to sauvignon blanc so constant monitoring by the viticultural and winemaking team ensures the grapes are picked under optimum conditions.

In 2009, the company launched a new range of wines to honour Ross. Appropriately called 'The Pioneer', these wines have been eagerly snapped up both in New Zealand and overseas. Lawson's Dry Hills continue to offer sauvignon blanc of exceptional complexity and consistency. Every wine is true to the company's guiding philosophy of creating premium Marlborough wines of singular character, quality and varietal expression.

LAWSON'S DRY HILLS SAUVIGNON BLANC
Inviting hints of peach and nectarine on the nose which are also echoed on the palate together with freshly torn basil. A ripe, full-flavoured style balanced with a fresh acidity offering the best of classic Marlborough sauvignon blanc.

Pacific-style Marinated Fish

WINE MATCH
Lawson's Dry Hills Sauvignon Blanc

500g skinned and boned white fish
½ cup lemon juice
¼ teaspoon salt
1 each: small green or red chilli, red pepper (capsicum), seeded
   and diced
1 small red onion, diced
4 tablespoons chopped coriander
½-¾ cup light coconut milk
salt and freshly ground black pepper to taste

Cut the fish into 2-3cm cubes. Combine with the lemon juice in a glass or ceramic bowl. Sprinkle with salt. Add a little water if there is not enough juice. Mix well. Refrigerate for at least one hour, until the fish takes on a cooked appearance.

Drain well. Combine with the remaining ingredients. Chill until ready to serve. **SERVES 6 AS A STARTER.**

Little Beauty

www.littlebeauty.co.nz

ittle Beauty quietly crept onto the local wine scene in 2008. Created as a special range of up-market wines for special, up-market places, Little Beauty offers a tiny but authentic taste of Marlborough to discerning UK diners at venues such as Claridges and The Savoy and Michelin-star restaurants including Andrew Fairlie at Gleneagles. It can also be found on the wine lists of Jamie Oliver's famed Fifteen, as well as Peter Gordon's Providores and at iconic locations such as London's National Theatre.

Little Beauty Sauvignon Blanc is made from grapes grown at a discrete, single vineyard site in the Waihopai Valley and is carefully hand-crafted by the talented and delightful winemaker, Eveline Fraser. The wine has been awarded gold, silver and bronze medals in a number of local and international competitions and also won the trophy for 'Best Overall New Wine' in the UK's Harpers Wine and Spirits Design Awards 2010.

LITTLE BEAUTY LIMITED EDITION SAUVIGNON BLANC
Subtle yet inviting aromas of minerals and citrus before a powerful palate with plenty of intense flavour. Lemon and lime embraced by a fine acidity giving the wine great structure. Pure and polished.

Mahi Cellar Door, Renwick

Mahi

www.mahiwine.co.nz

Nowhere will you find a more effusive and passionate man than Mahi's proprietor and winemaker Brian Bicknell. He exudes enthusiasm the same way that his wines exude a unique quality resulting from his care and nurturing.

Brian and his wife Nicola established Mahi in 2001, fulfilling a long-held dream. At the small, boutique winery in Renwick, purchased in 2006, Brian is hands-on with every aspect, working with a strong focus on single-vineyard wines and the objective of respecting and promoting the individuality of the various sites.

'One of the many things that we love about wine,' Brian explains, 'is that it is such a true reflection of its place. It is the way that it shows the differences between vineyards that was the inspiration for the start of Mahi. To make wines in as natural a way as possible from great vineyards is a constant enjoyment, and then to see these wines through to the bottle, watch them slowly evolve, and to enjoy them at the table with friends is incredibly satisfying.'

The team pride themselves on having minimal influence on the fruit, but take every precaution to ensure the grapes are pristine. Every variety goes down the 'triage table' to be hand-sorted, with only perfect fruit allowed to pass through.

Sauvignon blanc is the variety that is perhaps the most complex and most challenging for the Mahi team given the style they desire to create. They put much effort into fruit selection to ensure there is a wide range of components available for blending. By using hand-picked parcels, barrel-fermentation, wild yeasts and occasionally some malolactic influence, the result is a complex, rich style of sauvignon with great texture and length of flavour creating an ideal match with food.

Mahi, meaning 'our work, our craft' uses a symbol representing the strength, life and growth of the native New Zealand frond (fern), with the understanding that wine should never be rushed to bottle, respecting its ability to evolve naturally over time. Brian's sauvignon blanc is certainly one that will benefit from time in the bottle, gaining further nuances and complexity.

MAHI SAUVIGNON BLANC
Offering lifted aromas of juicy nectarine, this elegant wine shows a wonderful intensity of rich flavours and textures. Silky smooth and with a unique richness, the complexities are pleasing and rewarding. A wonderful food wine which will also reward a short period of cellaring.

Crayfish Salad with Mustard Aioli

WINE MATCH
Mahi Sauvignon Blanc

Mustard Aoili:
1 plump clove garlic, peeled and crushed
1 small egg yolk, lightly whisked
salt and white pepper to taste
1 tablespoon lemon juice
½ cup extra virgin olive oil
1 teaspoon wholegrain mustard

1 large crayfish, cooked
1 small Granny Smith apple, peeled, cored and diced
1 avocado, peeled, stoned and diced
1-2 tablespoons lemon juice
freshly ground salt and pepper to taste
1-2 teaspoons diced, char-grilled red pepper (capsicum)

To prepare the aioli, place the garlic, egg yolk, seasonings and lemon juice in a blender. Mix, until smooth. With the motor running, slowly drizzle in the oil in a steady stream. Continue mixing, until thick. Stir in the mustard.

To make the salad, pull the tail away from the crayfish and remove the flesh. Cut into cubes. Combine with the apple and avocado in a bowl. Sprinkle with a little lemon juice. Season.

Place the combined salad ingredients into the empty crayfish tail. Garnish with red pepper. Serve the aioli on the side. **SERVES 4 AS A STARTER.**

Mud House

www.mudhouse.co.nz

A highly successful and dynamic operation, Mud House has a choice of fruit from company vineyards and growers across the Marlborough region, giving the team plenty of options when it comes to fruit selection and blending.

Marlborough sauvignon blanc is the company's flagship with two styles produced – the ultra-premium estate single vineyard label and the Mud House itself. The latter is accessible, pleasing and highly enjoyable made from grapes grown in the Wairau, Awatere and Ure Valleys. The compelling single estate wine, The Woolshed Vineyard, offers a depth and complexity that reflects both the essence of the grape variety and that of the vineyard.

Sauvignon blanc is one of winemaker Nadine Worley's favourite wines to make and drink. 'Lift the lid on a tank and behind the yeast will be pungent aromas of tropical fruits and lifted nettles. That's when you know it's going to be good.'

MUD HOUSE MARLBOROUGH SAUVIGNON BLANC

A fresh and exhilarating wine with aromas of the sea – mineral tones combine with fresh, zesty fruit and a succulent mid-palate to give a rewarding wine with a dry finish. Brilliant to enjoy young while vibrant though it will gain in complexity.

The eye-catching steel and copper shell at Nautilus' Cellar Door

Nautilus

www.nautilusestate.com

A leader in the region's wine industry, Nautilus with its steel and copper shell sculpture outside the cellar door offers an eye-catching welcome to one of the region's finest producers. Nautilus employs a highly successful, loyal team which thrives on delivering quality and authenticity in every wine. Winemaker Clive Jones is a perfectionist and it shows. Research carried out by local academics has identified the different characteristics that make Marlborough sauvignon blanc so distinctive and Clive aims to encompass all of those different flavour compounds to give a wine that is complex and long-lasting.

Nautilus Sauvignon Blanc is made from grapes drawn from several vineyards including those in the Awatere Valley, Opawa, Renwick, Kaituna and Lanark Lane, just west of Renwick all hand-picked and whole-bunch pressed. Clive is passionate about sauvignon blanc and his philosophy is to make a style that embraces 'classic Marlborough' but in a more pure, polished format. 'It is great to taste the distinctive Marlborough sauvignon blanc flavours as they develop on the vine. Then we see them further emerge through fermentation and we can release a world-class product three months later. A wine that is truly made on the vine.'

In 2006, the company completed a new wine-making facility to process sauvignon blanc and other white varietals. This facility is state-of-the-art, allowing precise control of the winemaking process and improving the environmental footprint of the winery by reducing energy requirements and waste. The aforementioned nautilus shell sculpture was commissioned to celebrate the opening of this new facility and was created by Whanganui artist Dale Hudson, who had lived near the winery in Renwick and had specialised in artwork involving natural shapes. The sculpture comprises over one kilometre of stainless steel and copper wire and more than 1,000 spot welds.

Nautilus Estate Sauvignon Blanc is regarded as one of New Zealand's most consistent, premium quality wines. It has won trophies and gold medals in both national and international wine competitions and is exported to over 30 countries. Nautilus Estate is one of a handful of wineries licensed to use the prestigious New Zealand Fern brand.

NAUTILUS SAUVIGNON BLANC

Flinty, steely, mineral aromas paying homage to the great wines of Sancerre in France's Loire Valley. Freshly chopped summer herbs, a citrus freshness and ripe underlying orchard fruit flavours give a superbly balanced, delicious wine.

Chilli & Lime-dressed Oysters

WINE MATCH
Nautilus Sauvignon Blanc

1 teaspoon finely grated root ginger
¼ cup each: lime juice, white balsamic vinegar
1-2 teaspoons julienned chilli
½ teaspoon each: fish sauce, caster sugar
1 small shallot, finely diced
24 fresh oysters

Garnish:
1 tablespoon each: finely chopped chives, julienned chilli,
   small lime wedges

Combine the ginger, lime juice, vinegar, chilli, fish sauce,
caster sugar and shallot. Chill this dressing, until required.
Best prepared and served on the same day.

Place the oysters on serving plates and top with a little of the
dressing or serve on the side. Garnish with the chives, chilli
and lime.

Excellent served with small triangles of thinly sliced brown
bread. **SERVES 4 AS A STARTER.**

Opawa

www.opawawine.com

First produced in 2010, Opawa Sauvignon Blanc is made from grapes carefully selected from specific valley floor sites that offer a more tropical fruit spectrum. A small portion of barrel-fermented sauvignon is included to add complexity and texture without the more obvious oak character. The resulting wines hold great appeal and drinkability, shown by their quick acceptance in the market place, both in New Zealand and overseas.

Opawa means 'smoky river' in Maori and is named after the river that runs through the heartland of Marlborough. It begins in the Wairau Valley and flows through and around the eastern suburbs of Blenheim where it is crossed by the Opawa River Bridge. It joins the Taylor River in Blenheim (keeping the Opawa name) and flows into Cook Strait at Cloudy Bay, just south-east of the mouth of the Wairau River.

The contemporary appeal of Opawa reflects a new generation of sauvignon blancs that promote excellence, affordability and enjoyment while keeping a firm footing in the vineyard.

OPAWA SAUVIGNON BLANC
Lovely, fresh, pronounced aromas of sweet, ripe tropical fruits that make your mouth water in anticipation. Juicy and succulent with plenty of flavour, this is a gem of a wine. You can still taste it five minutes later.

Sacred Hill

www.sacredhill.com

Though based in Hawke's Bay, Sacred Hill has long had a love affair with Marlborough, producing some of the region's most highly recognised sauvignon blancs. Show successes have seen the Sacred Hill 'orange label' receive numerous gold medals, rewarding loyal followers with the guarantee of quality year in, year out.

Sacred Hill's principal Marlborough vineyard is called Hells Gate; the name is derived from an eerie gorge located at the headwaters of the Wairau River. Situated on the southern side of Marlborough's Wairau Valley, the 60-hectare vineyard is planted primarily with sauvignon blanc, and lies on the banks of the Omaka River on a sunny, stony river terrace that benefits from the fluctuations in temperature. Cool nights ensure that the characteristic flavours and aromas of Marlborough sauvignon blanc are retained as the grapes ripen in the sunny climate.

SACRED HILL SAUVIGNON BLANC
Lime cordial and 'wet stone' aromas, this is a dry wine that shows off the quality of the fruit. Polished, citrusy, mouth-watering and sinuous, ideal pre-dinner or with a number of light, subtly flavoured summer dishes.

Saint Clair

www.saintclair.co.nz

Saint Clair Family Estate was founded in 1978 by Neal and Judy Ibbotson, Marlborough viticulture pioneers. Grapes were originally supplied to local wine companies but in 1994 the family decided to launch their own label.

The company's mission is to create world-class wines that exceed their customers' every expectation and Neal with his viticultural expertise together with winemakers Matt Thomson and Hamish Clark certainly achieves this. The company excels at sauvignon blanc and with 12 Pioneer Block wines, plus the Wairau Reserve, Saint Clair Marlborough and Saint Clair Vicar's Choice, this is obviously where the passion lies. Frequent medal and trophy winners in wine competitions in New Zealand and abroad, these wines are a bold upfront expression of the sauvignon blanc grape.

Saint Clair has a classification system which evaluates the fruit and the resulting wines, ensuring only the best – and those with the desired characteristics – are chosen to contribute to each of the specific labels. All the different batches of grapes are kept separate in as many as 130 tanks and once fermented are assessed by the company's wine judging panel and given a quality-based score. This score determines into which tier the wine is blended. The team has learned a number of things from this system including that just as Marlborough sauvignon blanc is different to sauvignon blanc from other parts of New Zealand and the world, so are wines from the different subregions within Marlborough. Each has their nuances and characters that make them unique.

Saint Clair has identified that their best sauvignon blancs come from the lower Wairau Plain with its more fertile, deeper, free-draining and uniform soils. This area has become a favourite of winemaker Matt since 2001 when they produced just 2000 cases from here whereas in 2010 this had jumped to the equivalent of 100,000 cases with associated quality increases identified throughout all of the Saint Clair labels.

Saint Clair also uses this system as a method to determine the value of the grapes and therefore the grower payments. This results in a greater awareness of the effects of vineyard management techniques and encourages the desire to improve that management to the benefit of both the grower and Saint Clair.

This quality assessment system has also identified a unique subregion in the Ure Valley, 40 kilometers south of the main Wairau Valley, with high limestone content in the soil and with a similar climate. Saint Clair is producing Pioneer Block 4 Sauvignon Blanc from grapes grown here.

Neal and Judy's offspring are all

continued on pg 95

Saint Clair's cellar door in the vines at the corner of Rapaura and Selmes Roads

Saint Clair continued from pg 93

involved in this family-run business. Son Tony is responsible for the design of Saint Clair's packaging, promotional material and advertising through his design consultancy business in Sydney. Daughters Sarina and Julie are involved in sales and marketing after studying wine business marketing in Adelaide.

The company's wines can be found in 45 countries around the world and adorning some of the finest tables from the luxurious Emirates Palace in Abu Dhabi to the deluxe, five-star Claridges Hotel in London. In the last 10 years, Saint Clair sauvignon blancs have amassed a huge 66 trophies and 182 gold medals – that's an average of three gold medals and a trophy every other month.

SAINT CLAIR MARLBOROUGH SAUVIGNON BLANC

A big, powerful wine. The monster nose hits you at 40 paces – lots of passionfruit and sweaty characters, all echoed on the palate with an underlying sweetness from the ripe fruit. Textural and weighty with great length of flavour.

SAINT CLAIR PIONEER BLOCK 3 43 DEGREES SAUVIGNON BLANC

Big sherbet nose, intense, mouth-watering aromas leading to a full-flavoured, powerful wine with a firm acid structure and stacks of ripe, juicy fruit. Concentrated and long with lime, green apples and spice on the finish.

SAINT CLAIR WAIRAU RESERVE SAUVIGNON BLANC

Powerful, pronounced nose of passionfruit and sweet, juicy herbs, this big, expressive wine is weighty and textural. Flavours of fresh, succulent tropical fruit and a piercing leafiness leave a lasting impression.

Seafood Risotto

WINE MATCH
Saint Clair Wairau Reserve Sauvignon Blanc

3 tablespoons olive oil
1 each: onion, carrot, diced
2 cloves garlic, crushed
1 cup Arborio risotto rice
½ cup sauvignon blanc
4 cups fish stock
¼ teaspoon saffron threads
400g mixed seafood eg prawns, scallops, mussels, skinned and
    boned white fish, cubed
freshly ground black pepper to taste

Heat 2 tablespoons of the oil in a large pan over medium heat.
Add the onion and carrot and sauté for 3 minutes. Add the
garlic and sauté until soft and fragrant. Stir in the rice and heat
until the grains are shiny, about 1 minute. Add the wine and
simmer until it evaporates.

Bring the stock and saffron to the boil. Add a ½ cup to the rice
and bring to the boil, stirring constantly. Cook the rice, stirring
constantly, until most of the liquid is absorbed. Repeat using a
½ cup of stock each time, cooking until the rice is soft. Add the
seafood and heat, until cooked. Season.

Serve in wide bowls topped with chopped dill or fennel, if
preferred. **SERVES 4.**

Spy Valley

www.spyvalleywine.co.nz

Spy Valley Wines is situated on the Omaka River terraces on the south side of Marlborough's Wairau Valley. Bryan and Jan Johnson established the first of their 380 acres of estate vineyards in 1993, growing and supplying grapes to local winemaking companies. From vintage 2000 wine was produced and sold under the Spy Valley label. The brand name derives from a nearby satellite communications monitoring station, part of the Echelon Global Network.

Fruit for Spy Valley Sauvignon Blanc is grown on stony riverbed terraces. Once harvested, it is gently pressed then fermented in stainless steel tanks to preserve the intense passionfruit and gooseberry characters. The wine is fruit-driven in style, with complexity from lees ageing for several months before bottling and offers a classic example of Marlborough sauvignon blanc with intense flavours and a crisp acidity in a dry style.

Spy Valley also produce Echelon Sauvignon Blanc, an ultra-premium wine made from their oldest vines and given further complexity through oak treatment and maturation.

SPY VALLEY SAUVIGNON BLANC
Pronounced aromas of sweet, juicy, zesty fruits which are echoed on the palate of this appealing wine. Classic Marlborough sauvignon with the added bonus of length of flavour and true varietal definition.

Stoneleigh Sauvignon Blanc

www.stoneleigh.co.nz

Located in the heart of Marlborough's Rapaura region, the 178-hectare Stoneleigh vineyard is on the northern side of the Wairau River and within two kilometres of the bush-clad Richmond Ranges. The vineyards are located on deep, free-draining gravel beds covered in smooth stones. These stones have a special effect on Stoneleigh wines – they absorb the sun's heat during the sunny Marlborough days, and then reflect it back onto the vines at night, assisting ripening and contributing to an uplifting fruit-forward wine with lifted fresh aromatics.

Made from some of the region's oldest vines (20 years), fruit for Stoneleigh Sauvignon Blanc is harvested when the flavours reach their peak intensity and ripeness, whilst a minimalist winemaking approach helps the wine to express the best of the terroir. Famous for its vibrant, white nectarine and grapefruit aromatics with tropical passionfruit and subtle, sweaty notes, this wine is best enjoyed while it is young and exuberant.

For Stoneleigh's winemaker, Jamie Marfell, winemaking was an inevitable career choice. He grew up on a farm overlooking a valley of grapevines in Marlborough and his school holidays were spent planting or pruning vines, depending on the season. Following his studies in agricultural science and a postgraduate Diploma in Viticulture and Oenology at Lincoln University, Jamie began his career as a trainee winemaker in 1990. After some time spent travelling and gaining hands-on experience, Jamie returned to his hometown of Blenheim in 2002 to concentrate on crafting distinctive Marlborough Sauvignon Blancs. Jamie is passionate about this grape variety and believes the biggest challenge with sauvignon blanc is continually developing and differentiating the style.

Stoneleigh also makes the Rapaura Series Sauvignon Blanc – a premium, more intense, expressive wine with a layered complexity made using the best fruit from the Stoneleigh vineyard.

STONELEIGH SAUVIGNON BLANC
Hints of sherbet on the nose with elderflower and white currants leading to a more subtle, citrussy style of sauvignon blanc with underlying tropical notes. A good wine with food or to enjoy as a glass on its own, this is an easy style of wine with a huge following around the globe.

Broad Bean Salad with Mint & Feta

WINE MATCH
Stoneleigh Sauvignon Blanc

100g round beans, trimmed
500g (podded) broad beans
¼ cup mint leaves
75g feta cheese, diced or crumbled
3 tablespoons lemon juice
6-8 tablespoons extra virgin olive oil
flaky sea salt and freshly ground black pepper to taste

Blanch the beans separately in boiling water for about 2 minutes. Drain and refresh in icy water. Remove the skins from the broad beans.

Place in a serving bowl with the mint leaves and feta.

Whisk the lemon juice, olive oil, salt and pepper. Drizzle over the salad and serve. **SERVES 4.**

Sugar Loaf

www.sugarloafwines.co.nz

Established in 2004, Sugar Loaf Wines takes its name from the group of islands just off the dramatic Taranaki coastline where the company's founder, Kate Acland, grew up. After studying viticulture and winemaking at Lincoln University and a brief stint overseas, Kate came to Marlborough and set up Sugar Loaf Wines. In 2007 the opportunity arose to buy a disused apple-juicing facility and convert it into a small boutique winery.

Situated in the heart of Marlborough's wine-growing region, Rapaura, the winery is custom-built allowing ultimate control through every stage. Combining modern techniques and time-honoured traditions, Sugar Loaf aims to handcraft wines that truly represent the vineyards from which the fruit was sourced. The company's 20-acre vineyard is focussed solely on sauvignon blanc and is carefully divided into managed blocks based on soil types and character. Parcels of fruit are also selected from a small number of passionate growers in the Awatere and Wairau Valleys.

SUGAR LOAF SAUVIGNON BLANC
A dry wine with the fruit characters of typical, classic Marlborough sauvignon blanc. Lovely clean nose with tropical notes together with orchard fruits while the palate has a zippy acidity to balance the ripe fruit characters.

Te Whare Ra

www.tewharera.co.nz

TE WHARE RA SAUVIGNON BLANC
Grassy, lifted nose with pronounced elderflower and lime together with undertones of juicy, tropical fruit. Fleshy with a lovely vibrant acidity, this is a textural wine with a raft of concentrated, attractive flavours that last forever.

Ten Sisters Sauvignon Blanc

www.tensisters.co.nz

TEN SISTERS SAUVIGNON BLANC
Light nose, classic aromas, clean and inviting. A dry, aperitif style with good structure and ripe fruit together with fresh herbs on the finish. Ideal as a glass to enjoy on its own or with subtle-flavoured dishes.

Terrace Heights Estate

www.thewine.co.nz

THE NED

TERRACE HEIGHTS ESTATE SAUVIGNON BLANC

Lifted, bright, concentrated nose and a tasty, flavoursome palate. Summer herbs combine with a touch of passionfruit to give a well-made, appealing and rewarding wine. Tangy mineral aspects on the finish.

The Ned

www.marisco.co.nz

THE NED SAUVIGNON BLANC

Pears, herbs and green apples abound with this fresh and zesty wine. A clean and polished style with a lovely minerality on the finish. Medium-bodied and easy to enjoy, this popular wine denotes both varietal and vineyard influence.

The King's Favour

www.marisco.co.nz

Situated beside the Waihopai River on the southern side of the Wairau River, the 268-hectare Marisco vineyard is home to The King's Favour Sauvignon Blanc. This wine is one of several produced by proprietor and chief winemaker, Brent Marris, whose expertise and passion for sauvignon blanc clearly shows in each bottle.

It is not surprising that Brent has devoted much of his life to viticulture. He became the region's first born and raised qualified winemaker, graduating from Roseworthy Agricultural College (South Australia) in 1983 with a Bachelor of Applied Science in Oenology (winemaking). With more than 20 years grape growing, winemaking and marketing experience, he has a knack for creating brands and taking them to the world with significant success.

THE KING'S FAVOUR SAUVIGNON BLANC

Herbal expressions on the nose with an almost gentle creaminess indicating a richer style of wine. Full-bodied and weighty with plenty of flavour and subtle, tropical fruit undertones balanced with a fine, citrusy acidity. A smoother, more rounded style.

Tohu

www.tohuwines.co.nz

Tohu (pronounced Tor-who) is the world's first Maori owned wine company. Established in 1998, Tohu has been making its mark with wines produced from both Marlborough and Nelson.

As well as striving for varietal excellence with the added unique and distinct appeal of Maori legend, the wines are seen as a sign of the company's integrity as wine producers and therefore custodians of the rugged yet fertile soils of Aotearoa, the Maori term for New Zealand.

Tohu (meaning 'sign' or 'signature') true to Maori culture, has a strong spiritual connection to the land and therefore takes its responsibility to ensure this precious resource is passed onto future generations in pristine condition very seriously.

Tohu predominantly sources fruit from two vineyards owned and operated by the company, located in the Awatere and Waihopai Valleys. Grapes for the Mugwi label are sourced entirely from the Arapoto 'short path' block in the Awatere Valley vineyard. Naturally low yields from these vineyards and their distance from the moderating influence of the Pacific Ocean means the grapes offer concentrated fruit characters and are pristine with little or no disease pressure during the growing season.

In Maori culture, the koru or spiral symbolises growth, life and the natural world. The koru featured on the label comes from the painting *He Mihi Aroha Ki a Koe* by renowned Maori artist, Sandy Adsett. Sandy Adsett's koru is a classical motif from the kowhaiwhai depicted in his painting. Kowhaiwhai is the ancient Maori tradition of complex patterns. These symmetrical designs adorn the rafters of the elaborately carved Whare Tupuna

House of Ancestors and represent the voices of legendary heroes transmitting their wisdom through the ether.

In the spirit of this tradition, Tohu celebrates this iconic spiral. It represents the growth of the vines, the new life of the vines and the journey of New Zealand's people from the past to today. This koru signifies the long-term intergenerational goal for cultural, social, environmental and economic sustainability. In essence the koru has become the sign, or signature of Tohu.

The mountain silhouette featured by Tohu represents Mt Tapuae-o-Uenuku, the spectacular backdrop to the Awatere Valley vineyard. One of the highest peaks in New Zealand, Mt Tapuae-o-Uenuku dominates the inland eastern skyline, towering to 2,885 metres above sea level. In stormy weather the mountain is often framed by a double rainbow.

TOHU MUGWI RESERVE SAUVIGNON BLANC
A toasty rich nose from the extensive oak influence in this wine – lees influence also showing with a weighty texture along with tropical fruit flavours and some fresh acidity.

TOHU SAUVIGNON BLANC
An approachable, more subtle style of sauvignon with a delicate nettly, grassy character throughout the nose and palate. Fresh and balanced, ideal on its own or with light dishes such as salads or seafood.

Early morning sunrise casting light and warmth on to majestic Mount Tapuae-O-Uenuku, its silhouette and nobility a backdrop to the Tohu Awatere vineyard

Capsicums, Couscous & Goat's Cheese

WINE MATCH
Tohu Sauvignon Blanc

2 red peppers (capsicums)
4 teaspoons olive oil
1 small red onion, diced
2 cloves garlic, crushed
¼ cup each: boiling water, couscous, finely chopped wild rocket
4 sun-dried tomatoes, patted dry and diced
1 tablespoon capers
freshly ground black pepper to taste
100g goat's cheese, diced
1 medium tomato, sliced

Preheat the oven to 200°C.

Halve the peppers. Remove the seeds and ribs.

Heat 2 teaspoons of olive oil in a small pan. Sauté the onion and garlic, until soft.

Pour the boiling water over the couscous in a bowl. When the water is absorbed, stir with a fork.

Combine with the onion mixture, rocket, sun-dried tomatoes, capers and black pepper. Pack into the peppers. Top with the cheese and tomato slices. Drizzle with the remaining oil.

Bake for 20-30 minutes, until the peppers have softened. Serve hot or at room temperature. **SERVES 2.**

Twin Islands

www.twinislandswine.com

The name Twin Islands refers to the two largest islands of New Zealand. These are essential kiwi wines made by real kiwi characters to complement a kiwi lifestyle at the beach, at the bach, by the barbecue or on the boat.

The silver fern displayed on the label is a classic New Zealand waymark used by Maori to find their way through dense New Zealand bush.

Twin Islands is responsible for archetypal Marlborough wines, crafted with early and regular enjoyment in mind. Their clean, fresh and varietally distinctive palate ensures they fulfil this aim. First released in 1992, Twin Islands Marlborough Sauvignon Blanc offers an excellent value, full-flavoured wine. Fruit is sourced from selected vineyards in the Marlborough region all of which enjoy excellent ripening conditions for flavour development. Grapes are picked to ensure a balance of fresh and vibrant acidity.

TWIN ISLANDS SAUVIGNON BLANC
With a fresh, grassy, intense nose, this ripe and juicy pineapple fruit character wine is dry but deliciously fruit-driven. Plenty of succulent flavours all balanced with a crisp acidity. An easy, simple style that underlines all the classic hallmarks.

T

Villa Maria

www.villamaria.co.nz

Villa Maria is one of New Zealand's most successful wine producers. With a vast range of outstanding wines at every price point, the wine lover is constantly treated to gold medal and trophy-winning wines across the many styles.

The company's story is one of absolute passion. Villa Maria was founded by Sir George Fistonich and due to his dedication to quality the company became a New Zealand icon. From a young age, wine was a central part of his upbringing. 'Being Croatian, wine is in my blood. It's always been a part of life and I'm pleased to have spent my career pursuing this lifelong passion.'

Many things have changed since George won his first award at the Royal Easter Show in Auckland in 1962. The original half-hectare of grapes in Mangere, Auckland has developed into vineyards and wineries in four regions around New Zealand and wines produced from a dozen grape varieties are exported to 50 countries around the world. But he could not have imagined how far Villa Maria, and indeed the New Zealand wine industry would progress in the years to come.

From early on, Sir George focused on the importance of regional differences in relation to grape quality and wine styles. He pioneered the use of contract growers and Villa Maria became the first New Zealand wine company to initiate payment for grapes based on quality rather than a flat contract price.

In 2004, Sir George was short-listed as one of the 50 most prominent figures in the wine industry by UK *Wine International* magazine and in 2005 he was named New Zealand's Ernst & Young Entrepreneur of the Year.

Further kudos came in 2009 when Sir George received his greatest honour to date – a knighthood for his services to the New Zealand wine industry. He was one of only 85 to be knighted that year and the first to be acknowledged for services to the New Zealand wine industry. George became a Knight Companion of the New Zealand Order of Merit for his significant contribution to the industry and his history of national and international success.

In 2011 Sir George received a World Class New Zealander Award in the Manufacturing, Design & Innovation category and was also inducted into the New Zealand Wine Hall of Fame for services to the wine industry.

Quality and authenticity is the heart and soul of Villa Maria's range of wines and sauvignon blanc is no exception. From the top of the range Single Vineyard wines to the accessible Private Bin, every one is created with the utmost care and

continued on pg 111

Villa Maria's
Seddon vineyard

V

Villa Maria continued from pg 109

diligence under the watchful eye of both George and Group Winemaker Alistair Maling. The sauvignon blancs in the range are: Private Bin, Cellar Selection, Reserve, Single Vineyard and from the cellar door, the Research & Development Series, which gives the winemaker and viticultural team an outlet to try new techniques to showcase a forward-looking and innovative approach to winemaking.

VILLA MARIA CELLAR SELECTION SAUVIGNON BLANC

A dynamic, full-flavoured wine packed with fruit salad, green apples and lime. Fleshy texture and powerful, intense flavours which go on forever. A rewarding, richly-flavoured style that demands attention. Delicious.

VILLA MARIA PRIVATE BIN SAUVIGNON BLANC

Made from fruit selected from the Wairau Valley and the Awatere Valley, this wine offers a faultless experience of classic Marlborough sauvignon blanc. Ripe and zesty with crystal-clear varietal characters. A wine for any occasion.

VILLA MARIA RESERVE CLIFFORD BAY SAUVIGNON BLANC

The fruit for this wine comes from a variety of vineyards in the Awatere Valley which feature a spread of vine ages and viticultural techniques. Concentrated aromas of herbs, gooseberries and elderflower while the palate is underlined with a mineral-like, flinty character reflective of the terroir.

VILLA MARIA SINGLE VINEYARD SOUTHERN CLAYS SAUVIGNON BLANC

From the foothills of the Ben Morven Valley, this sheltered site covers a gentle north-facing slope and the vines are planted on some of the oldest clay soils in the region. The wine is richly tropical with passionfruit aromas and flavours balanced by a fresh, lime juice acidity. Outstanding.

Basil-infused Goat's Cheese

 **WINE MATCH**
Villa Maria Cellar Selection Sauvignon Blanc

¼ cup each; extra virgin olive oil, basil leaves, finely sliced
freshly ground black pepper to taste
200g soft goat's cheese
1 tablespoon basil pesto

Whisk together the oil, basil and black pepper.

Line a ¾-cup mould with plastic film. Spoon half the cheese into the mould and lightly press down. Spread with the pesto then top with the remaining goat's cheese. Pat down gently. Cover and refrigerate until ready to serve.

Upturn onto a serving plate. Remove the plastic film. Drizzle with the basil-infused oil.

Marinate at room temperature for at least 30 minutes before serving. Serve as a spread for breads or crackers. **SERVES 4.**

Bird watching on Wairau River Wines'
Home Block vineyard

Wairau River

www.wairauriverwines.com

Owned by the Rose family, Wairau River is one of the earliest growers of sauvignon blanc in Marlborough. Phil and Chris planted their first vines in 1978 growing for other producers before launching the Wairau River label in 1991. Situated on the corner of SH6 and Rapaura Road, the attractive cellar door and popular restaurant is a welcome haven for visitors and locals alike.

In 2002 a purpose-built 3,000 tonne winery was constructed, incorporating a state-of-the-art bottling line ensuring the highest degree of quality control could be exerted across all aspects of the winemaking process.

Now, all five of the Rose children are involved from the viticulture and winemaking side to finance, administration and the running of the restaurant.

The flagship wine is sauvignon blanc, made by Phil and Chris's winemaker son Sam who also makes a reserve sauvignon blanc. Both wines are in demand in New Zealand and overseas in the many markets that import and distribute the popular Wairau River range.

All the grapes are sourced solely from the company's own seven vineyards. Wairau River maintains a total commitment to quality by carefully managing these sites in order to keep yields low, thereby maximising quality, aromatics and flavour. Wairau River is one of the region's largest independent wine estates with a focus on making wines that are truly expressive of their Marlborough roots.

Wairau River takes sustainability and the environment seriously. The company undertakes the following practices: marc recycling – all the grape skins from the presses go straight onto the vineyards; the use of wind machines instead of helicopters to help with frost protection; recycling of empty spray containers; membership of Sustainable Winegrowing New Zealand; the planting of native trees and the conversion of an area within one of the company's vineyards for organic practices.

WAIRAU RIVER SAUVIGNON BLANC
Clean and fresh, the pungent aromas embrace ripe, tropical fruit, lemon zest and a touch of 'wet stone' minerality. Easygoing and enjoyable, this fruity style is a lovely example of good quality Marlborough sauvignon blanc.

Double-baked Blue Cheese Soufflé

WINE MATCH
Wairau River Sauvignon Blanc

*Based on a recipe
served at the
Wairau River Wines
Cellar Door &
Restaurant.*

75g butter
6 tablespoons plain flour
1½ cups milk
125g strong blue cheese, roughly chopped
1 tablespoon finely chopped parsley
freshly ground black pepper to taste
3 egg yolks
5 egg whites
¾ cup cream, approximately

Preheat the oven to 190°C. Lightly grease 6 x #1 (150ml) soufflé dishes.

Melt the butter, add the flour and cook on low heat for 1 minute. Gradually whisk in the milk, ensuring there are no lumps. Cook, stirring, until thick. Stir in the cheese, until melted. Mix in the parsley and pepper then the egg yolks.

Whisk the egg whites until they form soft peaks. Fold into the cheese mixture. Do not overmix. Pour into the soufflé dishes and place in a baking dish.

Pour hot water into the baking dish to reach halfway up the dishes. Bake for about 25 minutes or until risen and golden on top. Cool. Refrigerate, until required.

To serve, turn out the soufflés into shallow-sided dishes. Cover with a little cream. Bake at 190°C, until puffed and golden brown.

Great served with a rocket, sliced green apple and toasted walnut salad. **SERVES 6 AS A LIGHT MEAL.**

Wild South

www.wildsouthwines.co.nz

WILD SOUTH MARLBOROUGH SAUVIGNON BLANC

With juicy, sweet fruit on the nose with a hint of grassiness, this is a fresh and vibrant style with a pleasing sherbet acidity. Nice weight on the mid-palate with succulent fruit flavours including a hint of guava. A lovely, easy-going wine.

Wither Hills state-of-the-art winery and cellar door

W

Wither Hills

www.witherhills.co.nz

Wither Hills, named after the dramatic, barren ranges behind the winery on New Renwick Road, is a true success for the Marlborough wine region. Established in 1994 before building a state-of-the-art winery and cellar door in 2005, Wither Hills has a firm grasp on creating stylish wines with instant appeal.

Focusing on a polished representation of the grape variety and vineyard, the team works hard to ensure authenticity and quality are the priorities. With a big international team employed during vintage, Wither Hills provides a great place to learn about and make wine, while the customised sound system blasts out the latest music.

Chief Winemaker Ben Glover is both passionate and dedicated when it comes to making wine under the Wither Hills label. He started as a young boy training vines and bud-rubbing in his father's vineyard and from here his passion for wine grew. After finishing a marketing degree and postgraduate studies in oenology, Ben set out to gain practical experience overseas in Sonoma in California, Margaret River in Western Australia, Burgundy in France and Puglia in Italy. This wide-ranging experience gave Ben a raft of valuable knowledge across numerous wine styles and grape varieties, so when asked to be part of setting up Wither Hills he added significant value from day one.

Wither Hills Sauvignon Blanc comes in two distinct styles – Rarangi from a large vineyard site close to where the Wairau River joins Cook Strait and the Wairau Valley from company-owned vineyards and selected nearby growers. Planted in 2002, the Rarangi vineyard soils are a combination of what was coastal waters edge and natural wetland waterways. The Wairau Valley Sauvignon Blanc with its larger number of components contributed from various vineyard sites gives the winemaking team a wonderful array of wines to choose from when blending. The end result is a succulent, fruit-driven style with huge global appeal.

WITHER HILLS SINGLE VINEYARD RARANGI SAUVIGNON BLANC

Pungent and lifted, this vibrant style offers polished, ripe fruit and a refreshing, zesty acidity combined with an almost salty tang. Mineral aspects come through on the finish but in the main this is a mouth-watering combination of juicy citrus fruits and freshly chopped herbs.

WITHER HILLS WAIRAU VALLEY SAUVIGNON BLANC

A ripe, juicy and slightly sweeter style of wine that combines fresh lime, basil, herbs and lemon zest with a hint of minerality. Lush and fleshy with plenty of sweet, ripe passionfruit and grapefruit – a very enjoyable style.

Fresh Capsicum & Avocado Spring Rolls

WINE MATCH
Wither Hills Wairau Valley Sauvignon Blanc

1 avocado, halved, stoned peeled and thinly sliced
1-2 tablespoons lemon or lime juice
12 round rice paper wrappers
1 large red pepper (capsicum), seeded and julienned
1 cup each: thinly sliced iceberg lettuce, watercress
½ cup each: mint leaves, coriander leaves

Spicy Dipping Sauce:
¼ cup each: sweet chilli sauce, lime juice
1 teaspoon diced red chilli

Sprinkle the avocado with the lemon or lime juice.

Place 1 sheet of rice paper in a dish of warm water, until just softened. Place on a board.

Place 3-4 slices of the red pepper and a little lettuce and watercress on one edge of the wrapper. Add slices of avocado and a few mint and coriander leaves. Fold in the sides and roll up enclosing the filling. Place on a platter and cover with a damp paper towel.

Repeat until all the rolls are prepared.

Combine the ingredients for the dipping sauce and serve with the rolls. **SERVES 6 AS AN APPETIZER.**

Wetland ponds capture rainfall
for Yealands Estate vines

Yealands Estate

www.yealands.com

When Peter Yealands began planting on a grand scale in the foothills of the Awatere Valley many people were cynical and certainly curious. This was no small boutique producer, this enterprise was going to be a serious market player.

Yealands Estate Awatere vineyards stretch from the snow-capped Mt Tapuae-o-Uenuku and the Seaward Kaikoura Ranges all the way to the ocean at Clifford Bay. While enjoying low rainfall and high amounts of sunshine, these vineyards are also located in one of the windiest stretches of Marlborough. These elements plus the ruggedness of the land and the high amount of minerals in the soil produce distinctive and intense styles of wine. The two Wairau vineyards are closer to the township of Blenheim, at Grovetown and Riverlands and are planted exclusively in sauvignon blanc. The Grovetown site was once a marsh, but recognising its potential for growing quality grapes, Peter drained the land and developed the vineyard around an attractive wetland area.

Peter's vision from day one was all about sustainability and preserving and enhancing the environment so it wasn't surprising that the company was the first in New Zealand to be carboNZero certified. Every step of the way this has been the company's mantra with everything from vineyard management to packaging being carefully considered in order to minimise any potentially negative effect on the environment. Yealands Estate's certified carboNZero, means that the company's (already low) carbon footprint is totally offset by their investment in carbon credits.

The Yealands winery was created to blend into the landscape, becoming an unobtrusive and finally surprising structure as you draw closer. With no sharp edges cutting the skyline, this ergonomic and economical (in terms of its environmental impact) winery is possibly one of the most innovative anywhere in the world.

Some of the sustainable practices carried out by Yealands Estate include: the use of miniature babydoll sheep between the rows to lessen the need for sprays and tractors; wetland ponds capturing rainfall for release into the soil; the composting of grape marc; recovering and recycling of heat energy from refrigeration; solar reflective, high-insulation cladding; and the use of recycled glass and cardboard in packaging. They are also the first winery in the world to be using vine prunings as an energy source for the winery, burning them in place of LPG.

Happiest when pulling levers on large machines as he works the land, Peter Yealands' trademark 'can do' attitude has seen him succeed with a number of initiatives, all involving natural resources. Previous successful enterprises have included being the first to commercially farm greenshell mussels, leading to him

continued on pg 124

Y

Yealands Estate continued from pg 123

being granted the first marine farming license and being a catalyst for an industry now worth in excess of $160m in New Zealand export earnings. Peter also developed a deer farm on a 2,000 hectare property in the Marlborough Sounds (winning a major environmental award in 2003) and has successfully developed a number of vineyards including seven sites of his own and a number for other companies.

Yealands produces three styles of sauvignon blanc: Yealands Reserve only made in exceptional years, carefully crafted from small parcels of fruit from the Seaview vineyard in the Awatere Valley; Yealands Estate – a single estate wine made purely from Awatere fruit; and Peter Yealands – a fruit-driven style that offers appeal and enjoyment to lovers of Marlborough sauvignon blanc worldwide.

PETER YEALANDS SAUVIGNON BLANC

This fruit-driven wine is packed with tropical and stone fruits together with a hint of mineral 'wet stone' character. Dry, yet with the impression of sweetness from the ripe fruit, this wine is well-balanced and rewarding.

YEALANDS ESTATE SAUVIGNON BLANC

A fresh, herbaceous wine with a lifted, inviting aroma that leaps out of the glass. Full of flavour, ripe and rewarding with some nice intensity and rich texture on the mid-palate. A very easy style to sit back and enjoy, with or without food.

YEALANDS ESTATE RESERVE SAUVIGNON BLANC

With some time on yeast lees and a touch of oak influence, this wine shows a more mellow, richer style of nose and a weighty, mouth-coating palate. Dried herbs, honey and cashew nuts together with a hint of tropical fruit make this an excellent food wine – subtle and elegant.

Yealands winery and cellar door

Thai-style Green Pea Soup

WINE MATCH
Peter Yealands Sauvignon Blanc

1 tablespoon canola oil
2-4 tablespoons Thai green curry paste
500g peas
1 cup water
¾ cup light coconut milk
2 tablespoons chopped coriander

Heat the oil in a saucepan over medium heat. Add the curry paste and fry for 1 minute.

Add the peas and water. Simmer for about 5 minutes. Purée in a blender. Sieve, if preferred. Return to the saucepan.

Add the coconut milk and coriander and heat through. **SERVES 4.**

Tomato & Chilli Linguine

WINE MATCH
Yealands Estate Sauvignon Blanc

10 sun-dried tomatoes,
1-2 tablespoons olive oil
2 each: shallots, garlic cloves, finely diced
⅛-¼ teaspoon chilli flakes
8 cherry tomatoes, halved
flaky sea salt and freshly ground black pepper to taste
100g dried linguini, cooked
25g baby spinach leaves
50g feta cheese, diced
grated parmesan cheese to taste

Drain the sun-dried tomatoes and pat dry. Coarsely chop.

Heat the oil in a saucepan. Sauté the shallots and garlic, until softened. Add the chilli flakes and sun-dried tomatoes, heat through, then add the cherry tomatoes. Season. Toss together with the cooked pasta. When almost heated through add the spinach and feta.

Serve in bowls garnished with the parmesan. **SERVES 2.**

Y

Mini Red Pepper Palmiers

 WINE MATCH
**Serve with your choice of
Marlborough Sauvignon Blanc**

150g char-grilled red pepper (capsicum)
1 clove garlic, crushed
1 cup finely grated parmesan cheese
2 sheets ready-rolled frozen flaky puff pastry sheets, thawed but chilled

Preheat the oven to 200°C°. Line an oven tray with baking paper.

Chop the red pepper. Purée in a food processor with the garlic.

Sprinkle a ¼ cup of the cheese on the kitchen bench. Place a sheet of pastry on top pressing it lightly into the cheese. Spread the pastry with half of the red pepper purée. Sprinkle with another ¼ cup of cheese.

Fold in the 2 opposite sides of the square so they meet in the centre. Fold in the same sides of the pastry again to meet in the centre.

Fold 1 half of the pastry over the other. Cut the pastry crosswise into 1cm-thick slices. Repeat with the remaining pastry sheet.

Place cut-sides down on the baking paper-lined oven tray. Bake for about 15 minutes, until golden. Cool on a wire rack. Store in an airtight container. Reheat to serve. **MAKES ABOUT 30.**

Cheesy Olives

WINE MATCH
**Serve with your choice of
Marlborough Sauvignon Blanc**

These nibbles can be prepared ahead and refrigerated or frozen in an airtight container. Reheat in the microwave.

1¼ cups flour
150g butter
225g grated, aged cheddar cheese
60 stuffed green olives, well drained

Place the flour and butter in a food processor and blend to the consistency of breadcrumbs. Add the cheese and process for another minute, until the ingredients begin to bind. Knead the dough lightly, roll into a ball, wrap in film and refrigerate for 30 minutes.

Take 1 teaspoon of dough and mould it around each olive. Place on an ungreased baking tray. Chill for 1 hour. (These can be frozen at this stage.) Thaw before baking.

Preheat the oven to 200°C. Bake for about 15 minutes, until golden. Serve warm. **MAKES 60.**

Excellent accompanied by black olives and pepperdews.

Wasabi Fish Cakes

WINE MATCH
**Serve with your choice of
Marlborough Sauvignon Blanc**

500g skinned and boned salmon or white fish eg, snapper, monk fish
2 egg whites
1-2 teaspoons wasabi paste
2 kaffir lime leaves, julienned and chopped
1 tablespoon each: cornflour, grated root ginger
3 tablespoons chopped coriander
1-2 tablespoons canola oil

Wasabi Sauce:
¼ cup lime juice
1 tablespoon each: light soy sauce, fish sauce
1 teaspoon each: wasabi paste, caster sugar

Chop the fish into small (5mm) pieces. Combine with the egg whites, wasabi paste, lime leaves, cornflour, ginger and coriander. Mix well.

Form into 8 cakes. Use about 2 good tablespoons for each cake.

Heat the oil in a non-stick frying pan. Pan-fry the fish cakes in batches, about 1 minute each side, until cooked and golden.

Drain on paper towels. Place in a 100°C oven to keep warm until all the cakes are cooked.

Whisk the ingredients for the wasabi sauce together and serve in small bowls or dishes on the side.

Great garnished with fresh herbs, karengo or julienned and fried leek. Serve as a starter or light meal. **MAKES 8.**

Wine-marinated Clams & Salad

🍾 **WINE MATCH**
Serve with your choice of
Marlborough Sauvignon Blanc

1kg steamed clams (in their shells)

Wine Marinade:
½ cup extra virgin olive oil
¼ cup sauvignon blanc
2 cloves garlic
¼ teaspoon salt
½ teaspoon honey
1 tablespoon Dijon-style mustard
2 tablespoons finely chopped chives

Salad:
4-5 cups mesclun
½ small red pepper (capsicum), julienned

Drain the clams and place in a large plastic bag.

Whisk the olive oil and wine together. Chop the garlic and sprinkle with salt. Crush using the blade of a heavy knife. Mash to a paste. Whisk into the dressing with the honey, mustard and chopped chives.

Pour over the clams, moving them around until they are well coated. Refrigerate for at least 1 hour.

Arrange the salad ingredients on four serving plates. Top with the clams. Drizzle with a little of the strained Wine Marinade.
SERVES 4 AS A STARTER OR LIGHT MEAL.

Refried Bean Tostadas

WINE MATCH
Serve with your choice of Marlborough Sauvignon Blanc

Beans:
2 tablespoons olive oil
1 medium onion, chopped
1 teaspoon ground cumin
435g can refried beans
1 tablespoon chilli sauce

32 round Mexican-style corn chips
1 cup each: finely sliced iceberg lettuce, grated feta or tasty cheddar
    cheese, diced tomato
½ cup each: sour cream, Mexican-style tomato salsa, coriander
1 avocado, stoned, peeled and sliced
1 lime cut into wedges

Prepare the beans by sautéing the onion in oil in a heavy frying pan, until softened. Add the cumin and cook for 30 seconds. Add the beans and chilli sauce and warm through. Cover and keep warm.

Meanwhile, place the corn chips in the oven or microwave to warm through. Place in a circle on four serving plates as a base for the topping.

Top with the warm beans, lettuce, cheese, tomato, sour cream and salsa and coriander. **SERVES 4 AS A LIGHT MEAL.**

Ten Tips
for Matching Food with Marlborough Sauvignon Blanc

'Savvy' is a fruit-filled, flavoursome, food-friendly wine, which enhances and complements numerous dishes.

1 Ensure that the food and wine flavours harmonize with each other – that they are balanced – rather than one being dominant.

2 Pick one or two of the stronger highlights in the food or wine and match it with like flavours.

3 Match light wines with light dishes and more robust savs with stronger flavours.

4 Identify the ingredients in the recipe that are up front in flavour. Pair the wine with these, not necessarily the main ingredient for example, chicken. A sauce often dictates which style of sauvignon blanc to choose.

5 Matching a 'savvy' with spicy food helps tame the heat of the food and allows the fruit flavours of the wine to shine through.

6 Sweetness in a dish – found, for example, in many Asian dishes – can increase the perception of acidity and tannin in a dry wine. The dish may benefit from a dash of lemon juice.

7 You can also sharpen rich dishes with a little lemon or lime juice.

8 Want to serve a favourite sav tonight? Then 'tweak' the recipe to match the wine.

9 In general, foods to avoid serving with sauvignon blanc include red meat, pickled vegetables, very salty dishes and recipes with large amounts of cream.

10 **Taking all of the above into account, generally:**
   - Choose lightly cooked shellfish such as prawns, oysters and grilled fish to match with minerally sauvignon blancs.
   - Citrussy savs are great with fish and chips, grilled chicken (without too much marinade) and Greek and Mexican dishes.
   - Grassy and herbaceous savs match well with asparagus, green peppers, herbs and dishes with lime, coriander and chilli.
   - Oaked sauvignon blancs marry well with veal and chicken – especially if served in a light creamy sauce – or with pasta dishes.

And remember, if you like the match – even if unusual – it works.

Hints

Weights & Measures
Recipes in this book use standard, level, metric measurements.

In New Zealand, England and the USA 1 tablespoon equals 15ml. In Australia, 1 tablespoon equals 20ml. The variation will not normally greatly affect the result of a recipe apart from with some bakes and cakes.

If preferred, use 3 teaspoons rather than 1 Australian tablespoon for measures of raising agents and spices.

Grams to Ounces
These are converted to the nearest measurable number.

grams		ounces
25	=	1
50	=	2
75	=	3
100	=	3.5
125	=	4
150	=	5
175	=	6
200	=	7
225	=	8
250	=	9
275	=	10
300	=	10.5
325	=	11
350	=	12
375	=	13
400	=	14
425	=	15
450	=	16
1kg = 1000g	=	2lb 4oz

Abbreviations
Metric

g	grams
kg	kilograms
mm	millimetre
cm	centimetre
ml	millilitre
°C	degree Celsius

Oven Setting Equivalents (To Nearest 10°C)

	Fahrenheit	Celsius	Gas regulo No
Very cool	225-275	110-140	1/4-1
Cool	300-325	150-160	2-3
Moderate	350-375	180-190	4-5
Hot	400-450	200-230	6-8
Very hot	475-500	250-260	9-10

Cup & Spoon Measures
(to nearest round number)

	Metric
¼ cup	60ml
½ cup	125ml
1 cup	250ml
2 cups	500ml
4 cups	1000ml or 1 litre
1 teaspoon	5ml
1 dessertspoon	10ml
1 tablespoon	15ml
2 teaspoons	1 dessertspoon
3 teaspoons	1 tablespoon
16 tablespoons	1 cup

Measures of Length

cm		approx. inches
0.5	=	¼
1	=	½
2.5	=	1
5	=	2
15	=	6
18	=	7
20	=	8
23	=	9
25	=	10
30	=	12

Alternative Names
In the English-speaking world, many culinary terms and names of foods cross national borders without creating confusion. However, some may need explanation.

caster sugar	castor sugar/ fine granulated sugar/superfine sugar
coriander	cilantro/Chinese parsley
cornflour	cornstarch
crayfish	rock lobster
eggplant	aubergine
flour	plain flour/all-purpose flour
frying pan	skillet
grill	broil
minced meat	ground meat
peppers	capsicums/sweet peppers
rocket	arugula/roquette
sieve	strain
spring onions	scallions/green onions
to stone	pit
tomato paste	concentrated tomato paste
tomato purée	tomato sauce (USA)

THE
MARLBOROUGH
WINE TRAIL

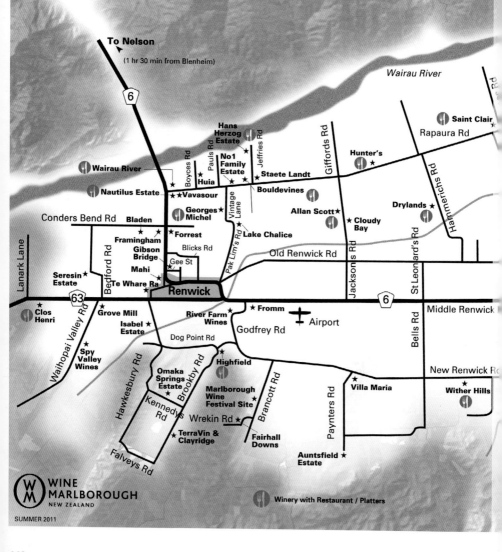

To Nelson
(1 hr 30 min from Blenheim)

Wairau River

6

Saint Clair

Rapaura Rd

Hans Herzog Estate

Jeffries Rd

Giffords Rd

Hunter's

Hammerichs Rd

Wairau River

Boyces Rd

Pauls Rd

No1 Family Estate

Staete Landt

Huia

Bouldevines

Drylands

Nautilus Estate

Vavasour

Vintage Lane

Allan Scott

Conders Bend Rd

Bladen

Georges Michel

Cloudy Bay

Lake Chalice

Framingham

Pak Lim's Rd

Forrest

Lanark Lane

Bedford Rd

Gibson Bridge

Blicks Rd

Old Renwick Rd

Jackson's Rd

St Leonard's Rd

Gee St

Mahi

Seresin Estate

63

Te Whare Ra

Renwick

6

Middle Renwick

Clos Henri

Waihopai Valley Rd

Grove Mill

River Farm Wines

Fromm

Airport

Bells Rd

Isabel Estate

Godfrey Rd

Dog Point Rd

Spy Valley Wines

Hawkesbury Rd

Omaka Springs Estate

Brookby Rd

Highfield

New Renwick Rd

Kennedys Rd

Marlborough Wine Festival Site

Brancott Rd

Villa Maria

Paynters Rd

Wither Hills

Wrekin Rd

Fairhall Downs

Falveys Rd

TerraVin & Clayridge

Auntsfield Estate

WINE MARLBOROUGH
NEW ZEALAND

SUMMER 2011

Winery with Restaurant / Platters

★ Johanneshof Cellars

Speeds Rd

Para Rd

(1)

To Picton
(30 min from Blenheim)

Tuamarina

Selmes Rd

O'Dwyers Rd

Spring
Creek

The Wine ★
Room

Thomson's
Ford Rd

Grovetown

Murphys Rd

Dodson St

Grove Rd

Nelson St

k Rd

Blenheim i-Site and
Railway Station

Battys Rd

High St

Mud House★

Main St

Blenheim

Malthouse Rd

Alabama Rd

Rd

★ Lawson's
Dry Hills

Redwood St

Mt Riley
Wines
★

Brancott ★

Riverlands

(1)

To Awatere Valley
(See Inset Map A) ▼

To Christchurch
▼ (3 hr 30 min - 4 hr from Blenheim)

0   5km

Cloudy Bay

★ **Awatere
River
Wines**

Ugbrooke Rd

20km to
Blenheim
▲ Lintons Rd

Redwood Pass

Reserve Rd

Awatere River

Yealands
Estate ★

Awatere
Valley Rd

Seddon

Seaview Rd

▼ To Chch   Inset Map A

𝒩

Recipe Index